Pacific War

Pacific War

New Zealand and Japan

1941–45

Second Edition

Matthew Wright

Intruder Books

This book is copyright and subject to international treaties.
No part may be copied, reproduced, or otherwise duplicated by any means, without prior permission of the copyright holder.

Copyright © Matthew Wright 2003, 2015 and 2018

The moral rights of the author have been asserted.

Maps copyright © Matthew Wright, 2003 and 2018
Cover photography copyright © Matthew Wright 2003

Published by Intruder Books, Wellington, 2018

ISBN 978-0-908318-20-9 (Intruder Books)

Publication history
First published 2003 by Reed New Zealand Ltd
Republished with minor revisions for Kindle 2015 by Intruder Books
Republished as a second edition in print 2018 by Intruder Books

The cover features a hinomaru yosegaki ('Good luck flag') picked up on Green Island Group in early 1944, author collection

This book is part of the New Zealand Military Series. Collect the set.

www.matthewwright.net
www.mjwrightnz.wordpress.com
www.facebook.com/MatthewWrightNZ

Contents

Introduction 1

1　The Road to War 3
2　Desperate Defence 25
3　Into the Islands 41
4　Guadalcanal to Green Islands 66
5　Tides of War 91

Epilogue: The Legacy of War 109

Notes 113
Glossary 127
Bibliography 129
Index 135

REVIEW COMMENTS ON THE ORIGINAL EDITION

"New Zealand changed in so many ways during and because of the Pacific war and this publication brings this out so clearly...a good book for history students and ideal to have in the family library."

– Alan Harris, *The Marlborough Express*, 23 September 2003.

Introduction

In December 1941, Japan attacked the British Empire and the United States, turning the European war that had raged since 1939 into a global conflict. For a few desperate months during early 1942, the Kiwis faced a deep crisis. Australia had its own threat to face. Britain was stretched to the utmost against Germany, and the United States — with millions still unemployed — took time to turn its huge industry to war production.

Despite a heavy commitment to the European war, New Zealanders eventually fought the Japanese on land, sea and air, from Malaya to the Solomons and, finally, in Japanese home waters. Kiwis also contributed in many other ways, providing bases and recreation facilities for US forces, food for the whole campaign, even sending physicists to work on the atomic bomb project.

This was not easy. New Zealand had heavy commitments in North Africa and Europe. Even after the crisis of 1942 had passed, the country struggled to find the resources to keep air force, navy and army operating in the Pacific. New Zealand's land component was finally withdrawn in 1944 after ongoing manpower issues reached crisis point — an issue that soon became entwined with Pacific politics and New Zealand's role in the war.

This book is one of a series of short titles, limited to about 35,000 words, that I wrote originally in 1999-2003 for Reed New Zealand. This 2018 print edition has been significantly revised.

Matthew Wright
September 2018

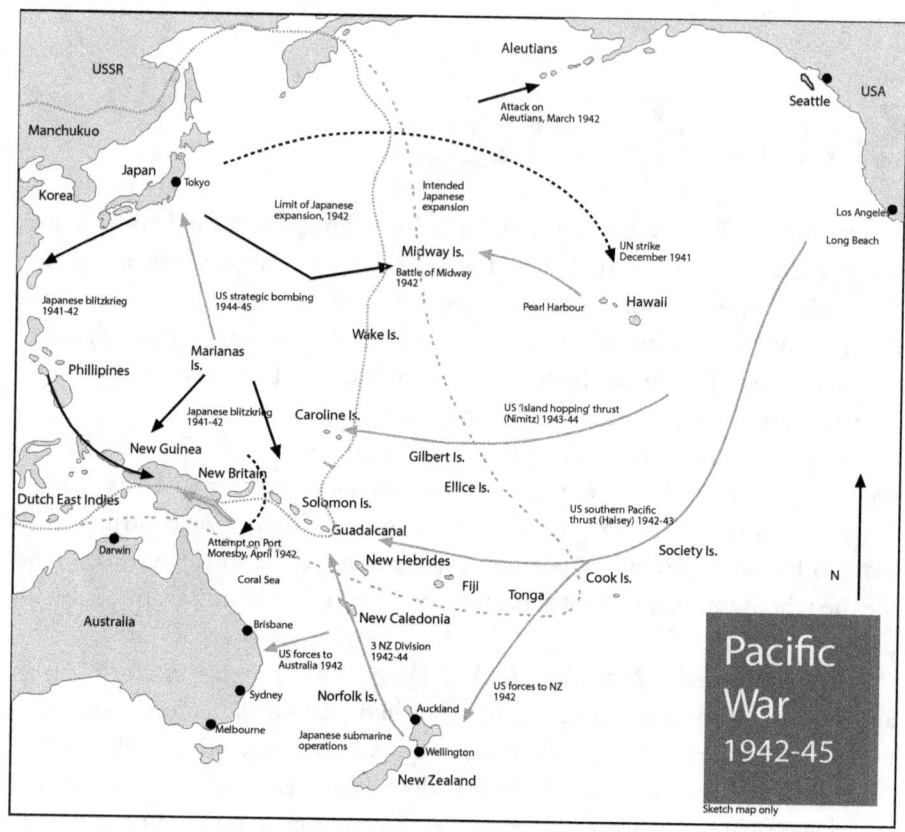

CHAPTER ONE
The Road to War

For the first time in our country's history we are directly threatened by enemy attack, and, at such a time, I am proud to say, the peoples are neither dismayed nor are they unaware of the perils and difficulties which may be in store for them.
— New Zealand Prime Minister Peter Fraser, 30 December 1941[1]

Total war came to New Zealand in December 1941, drawing civilians and combatants alike into the gravest crisis the country had ever faced. The nation had been at war with Germany since September 1939 — a conflict on which New Zealand's future pivoted, but which was physically remote. All that changed when Japan attacked the United States and the British Empire. For a few desperate months nothing seemed able to stop the forces of the 'rising sun'. The US Pacific Fleet was in ruins; the British 'Force Z' lay at the bottom of the South China Sea; and Singapore, the linchpin of New Zealand's security thinking for nearly two decades, fell just days after Japanese forces arrived on its doorstep.

New Zealand seemed isolated and vulnerable. There were plenty of men under arms from Kaitaia to Bluff, but they had little equipment and the RNZAF had no modern aircraft with which to deflect nuisance raids or tackle any invasion force.

Reaction varied. Most accepted the prospect of invasion stoically. Others were alarmed. Some panicked. One Auckland woman apparently even considered killing her children rather than let them fall into the hands of Japanese soldiers; but official reaction was more sensible. Local bodies pushed the Emergency

Precautions Service along and wondered about ways to evacuate the main centres.[2] The Labour government of Peter Fraser — privy to US intelligence analysis — believed invasion was unlikely, but certainly feared isolation, and with it starvation. New Zealand, one of the biggest food producers in the South Pacific, relied on imported fuel to run its farms, factories and transport networks. Japan had merely to block the essential sea links, and hunger would swiftly follow in the towns and cities.[3]

War Plan Orange and the Japanese threat 1905–36

Few were surprised by the Japanese attack of late 1941. Most participants thought war inevitable by that time; the immediate crisis had been building for nearly two years, and the wider oppositions around which it was fought had been well established for decades. The real origins of the struggle can be traced back to the late nineteenth century, when the West broke Japan's self-imposed isolation and the medieval world of the Tokugawa Shoguns was dragged, kicking and screaming, into the industrial age.

The main architects of change were Britain and the United States — the 'godparents of the new Japan', as British Prime Minister Sir Winston Churchill later put it.[4] The Meiji government that came to power in 1868 made swift adjustments. 'The old and new societies,' Churchill observed, 'with the chasm of ages between them, were intermingled and reacted upon each other in ways that no foreigner could understand.'[5] The resulting mix was incomprehensible to Westerners, a point that coloured associations up to and during the Second World War.

Japanese focus on *fukoku* (technological strength) and kyohei (military power) in an age of worldwide imperialism soon caused trouble.[6] There was war with China in 1886, opposition to Russian interests in Korea and, after 1898, a clash of interests with the United States in the Philippines. America was worried; but Britain — whose Chinese and South Pacific interests were threatened by Russia — sought friendship, ending 90-odd years of 'splendid isolation' in 1902 by concluding an alliance.[7] This did not allay fears in Australia and New Zealand. Nationalist ideology of the day was tied with racial stereotypes, and both Dominions feared uncontrolled Asian migration. This was a major factor behind an explicit 'keep Australia white' policy. Although originally directed at China, the thinking was easily transferred to Japan.

These fears assumed a military dimension in 1904 when Japan and Russia came to blows, and the Japanese swiftly delivered a drubbing to their vastly larger enemy.[8] As one Sydney paper remarked, 'it would be long before Asiatic power could so grow as to threaten the territory of Europe ... but Australia is a lonely outpost of the white race on the very borders of Asia'.[9] Opinion in New Zealand was less alarmist; Sir Robert Stout felt the real threat was economic.[10] But his was a lone voice. Sentiments in the United States also reflected prevailing ideas of race, and after anti-Asian riots in San Francisco during 1907, the US navy entered the fray with 'War Plan Orange' — a scheme to win a war with Japan by deploying the Pacific Fleet to the Philippines. The idea was tested the following year, and the Prime Ministers of both Australia and New Zealand invited the 'Great White Fleet' to visit, en route, amid clamorous popular applause.[11] 'As the champions of white ascendancy in the Pacific,' the *Evening Post* opined, 'America ... represents the ideals of Australia and New Zealand far better than Britain has hitherto been able to do.'[12]

The racial prejudices of the day were clear in such words; but at the time the more awkward side of such thinking was the fact that the mother country was allied to Japan. Australasian attitudes, repeated in the media, were an embarrassment to the Foreign Office in an age when Britain was implicitly looking to Japan to help secure its vast Pacifc interests against potential European rivals, a situation in which Germany was increasingly looking like a competitor. Nor did the problem go away; Australasian pressure for local naval defence, tacitly but obviously directed at the Japanese, caused a political headache for Britain, and although a compromise was reached in 1909, these diverging perceptions were not fully resolved until after the First World War.[13] By the time that war ended, United States objections to Japanese intervention in the Chinese Civil War had raised the stakes, and a new naval race was in full swing in which Japan seemed determined to build a significant fleet. This, inevitably, was viewed as a challenge to US interests in the western Pacific, and their own naval construction was revised to suit. Britain was unable to follow. The so-called 'war to end all wars' had virtually bankrupted the Empire and created, for the first time in decades, a deep ground swell of public sentiment for peace. In July 1921, Britain proposed an international disarmament conference to settle both the naval race and issues stemming from the Anglo-Japanese Treaty, which was up for renewal and under further strain as a result of British alignment with the United States.[14]

The Americans agreed to host the conference in November. What emerged was the first effective arms limitation arrangement in history — the so-called

'Washington Treaty' defining new naval limits. Japan, rather grudgingly, took second place behind Britain and the United States. A separately negotiated Pacific Treaty replaced the Anglo-Japanese alliance, defining the interests of the signatories in their Pacific Island territories.[15] None of these were wholly satisfactory; as one historian has noted, Japan was not deceived by the 'empty' Pacific Treaty, which was merely a 'device … for winding up an alliance'.[16] The 5:5:3 capital ship ratio, to which Japan agreed in exchange for British and United States agreement not to extend their naval basing beyond Singapore and Hawaii, became a source of resentment in Japan.[17]

One unexpected side-effect of the treaty flowed from the fact that it limited all major warship types, but the scale of those limits was such that a new 'arms race' shortly emerged, around the treaty limits as they applied to cruisers. The issue here was that Japan interpreted those limits fairly generously and embarked on a policy of specifically out-classing any potential rivals, with the result that the Imperial Japanese Navy ended up with a significant number of fast and powerful heavy cruisers that were difficult for western nations to counter at a time when naval air power was still in its infancy.

For Britain, however, the treaty cut-backs merely formalised an existing reality; the country could neither support the huge fleet it had built up during the First World War, nor embark on the expensive naval race that followed. Strategies for imperial defence with a reduced navy had been developed in late 1920, involving a defensive war in the Far East until the fleet could be brought through. This became the linchpin of New Zealand security thinking — though government did not buy into it wholesale until 1927, when Prime Minister J.G. Coates committed £1,000,000 to the Singapore naval base.[18]

United States schemes changed little. The Naval War College revised War Plan Orange several times, but the theme remained the same. The plan was predicated on the assumption that Singapore and Malaya would stand for at least three months; and the British, in turn, expected to be able to hold on largely because the American advance would threaten Japanese oil supplies from South East Asia.[19]

These precautions were not without justification. Japan's constitution prevented a government being formed without army and naval offers in cabinet, and policies were subordinated to the dictates of services which were in bitter rivalry. Politics in the early 1920s seemed progressive; but trouble began in 1927 when 36 banks collapsed amid new economic trouble. They took down many small industries and the Wakatsuki government with them, and the zaibatsu industrial-military complex took advantage of the chaos to reinforce its own power.[20] For a while Japan was in dire straits. The old standby of a foreign venture to take the heat off internal problems did not take long to emerge, and Japanese forces intervened at Shantung that year. They did so again in 1928. Hamaguchi Osachi became Prime Minister the following year and seemed more moderate, but Japan — racked by depression and food shortages — was ripe for revolt, and many in authority viewed military expansion as the answer. Hamaguchi was assassinated in 1930. Japan also came out ahead in the horse-trading that preceded the London Naval Treaty the same year, a point that caused alarm in New Zealand and Australia.[21]

Japanese politics remained prey to military demand. A coup was abandoned only at the last minute in 1931. When a Japanese railway in Manchuria was bombed, the Japanese Kwantung army used the event as a pretext to occupy the province without explicit political authorisation from Tokyo. International fears intensified in 1933 when the Japanese government — under the influence of the *Tosei-ha* (control school) military faction — withdrew from the League of Nations. A special Committee of Imperial Defence was formed under Major-General W.L.H. Sinclair-Burgess to co-ordinate New Zealand's response. The *Tosei-ha* gained influence over the cabinet of Hirota Kokai in early 1936, and in August that year the government declared new 'principles of national policy', including a rejection of treaty limits on naval power, and a plan to stop Soviet expansion into Asia. Half the state budget went on military spending that year amid talk of a 'quasi-wartime' economy.[22] The navy gained particularly; it was politically on the upswing in wake of a failed army coup the year before, and able to push ongoing modernisation along with a new building programme,[23] which included the two largest battleships ever built.[24]

China remained a focus of Japan's foreign interests. The Kuomintang government of Chiang Kai-shek tried to reach an agreement with Tokyo in 1935, even offering to recognise occupied Manchuria. The offer was rebuffed, and a minor incident in July 1937 used as a pretext for what became an undeclared war, in spite of the Japanese army's desire to remain aloof until it had built its strength. The so-called 'rape of Nanking' — an extraordinarily violent attack on Chiang Kai-shek's capital and its people — escalated the conflict, and by December 1937 Japan was embroiled in a full-scale conflict. When world attention was drawn to Europe by the Munich crisis in late 1938, Japan attacked Canton and declared a new Asian order.

In New Zealand these developments added to the sense of danger created by a resurgent Germany.[25] Hints from Britain that the 'main fleet' might take 70 days to reach Singapore and that deployment might be affected by a simultaneous war with Germany, were not encouraging.[26] The Pacific threat was laid over the European foundation — where Britain, potentially without France, faced growing German and Italian fleets. Nor could the United States offer succor. By the late 1930s, the US military was run down, and although war planning revolved around co-ordinated schemes for a two-ocean war, incorporating Orange, there were insufficient forces to fight in both theatres. The die was finally cast in 1938 when the British cabinet rejected proposed naval programmes, effectively guaranteeing that the Royal Navy would shortly not be strong enough to both fight in Europe and send the promised fleet to Singapore.

Whether Germany and Japan were a joint threat was another matter. The Anti-Comintern Pact of 1936 was not an alliance, and Japanese navy opposition killed an effort by the army to formalise an association with Germany in 1939. Japanese opposition to the Soviet Union in Siberia — along with the 120-day Nomonhan 'incident' that year, actually an undeclared war between Japan and the Soviets — stood uneasily beside Germany's non-aggression pact with Stalin.[27] That did not reduce the threat posed in the Pacific by Japan alone.

All these factors helped push New Zealand defence thinking in new directions during the late 1930s, although the process was neither wholly causal nor clear cut. Schemes for Pacific defence emerged in part from new focus on the RNZAF, which had been developed by the Savage administration in 1936–37 as a cheaper alternative to naval power.[28] Plans developed by the British-sourced Air Vice Marshal Ralph Cochrane called for far-ranging air reconnaissance from Fiji. These ideas were extended and developed through 1938 to include all the services, and efforts were also made to draw Australia into what was developing into a regional defensive scheme. These approaches emerged against a background of changing British policies, which suggested a wartime focus on the Mediterranean rather than the Far East and contributed to a New Zealand government decision in May 1938 to request a Pacific Defence Conference.

This conference was eventually held in Wellington during April 1939, attended by British, New Zealand and Australian delegates, each with their own agenda — the British wanted New Zealand to provide more pilot training facilities.[29] The prospect that the British might not be able to send a fleet was raised and discussed, but British delegates felt that while Singapore stood, New Zealand would face only raids. What emerged was a plan for a joint New Zealand and Australian patrol line from Port Moresby in New Guinea to Tongatapu in Tonga, using aircraft based at Port Moresby and Suva. The New

Zealand cabinet accepted most of the recommendations in May, though war in Europe — and with it, heavy calls on New Zealand's resources — came before work could begin on the Fijian airfield facilities, and the first strip at Nadi was not ready until early 1940.[30] The arrangement also did not imply land forces, which the Fijian government was still pursuing in July.[31]

Japan moves south, 1939–41

The European war that broke out in September 1939 did not immediately affect the Pacific, and for a while the Asian crisis developed independently. The United States terminated its Treaty of Commerce with Japan that year, and in December declared formal opposition to Japanese hegemony in Asia. The following year Japan began fortifying the Marshall Islands, to which US President Franklin D. Roosevelt responded by deploying the US Pacific Fleet to Pearl Harbor.

These tensions underpinned discussions between US Chiefs of Staff and British representatives, who met in late March 1940 to thrash out possible joint strategies. The results shaped the WPL-46 war plan, generally known as Rainbow-5, which was formally adopted by the United States in May, and envisaged a holding strategy in the Pacific while Germany was dealt with. No action was considered south of the equator other than protection of sea lanes, a change from earlier incarnations when Australia and New Zealand were waypoints during the drive west.[32]

At that stage Japan was not an immediate threat; nor could the hawkish Roosevelt overcome isolationist sentiment in Congress. That changed in May when Hitler's forces stormed through the Low Countries and France. From New Zealand's perspective the consequences were immediate. Apart from the direct threat to the 'mother country', the loss of the French fleet and Italy's entry into the war changed the balance of power at sea, forcing the British to formally suspend the Singapore strategy. This came just as the former French colonies in South East Asia became vulnerable to Japanese depredation. An alarmed Fraser cabled Churchill. While New Zealand's government did not:

> ...in any way demur to this decision ... [they] must observe that the undertaking to despatch an adequate fleet to Singapore, if required, formed the basis of the whole of this Dominion's defence preparations. They assume that this undertaking will again be made operative as soon as circumstances may allow, and they would most

earnestly request that the whole situation should be reviewed if the position in the Far East should become threatening…[33]

The United States, again, seemed a possible saviour, and Fraser proposed to match an Australian initiative, sending a minister to Washington 'in the hope of strengthening the security of the Pacific and of reinforcing the representations already made to President Roosevelt…'[34] Churchill disagreed; it might be misinterpreted as an attempt to influence domestic US politics. Roosevelt was pro-British, but Congress were not, and Churchill had to tread a delicate path. From Fraser's perspective the decision drove home the practical point that when push came to shove, New Zealand was not high in the Imperial pecking order, in which case US support was something to be cultivated.

In fact, American sentiment was already changing, and dramatically – a shift impelled by the fall of France, which gave Roosevelt leverage. He shortly obtained authorisation from an alarmed Congress for massive military spending. Legislation variously passed in June and July 1940 authorised the largest military build-up in United States history to that time. These included a massive naval construction programme covering the full range of warship types. New army divisions were projected, and orders were also placed for some 15,000 naval aircraft alone — a decision indicating that the vital role of air power at sea was thoroughly understood by US planners, well before Pearl Harbor, Coral Sea and Midway. Other initiatives included a project to develop huge multi-engined bombers capable of trans-Atlantic missions, as an explicit hedge against the fall of Britain. None of this could be achieved overnight – and many of the programmes that followed were not expected to reach full swing until 1943-44. But it meant that when war did come at the end of 1941, the United States was already re-arming.

The German victory in Europe created a power vacuum in the former French colonies of Indo-China, and with it an opportunity for Japan to encircle Chinese forces from the south. The alarmed but impotent Vichy French government had little option but to bend to pressure from the new government of Prince Konoe Fumimaro and allow Japan to use Indo-Chinese air bases.[35] A weakened Britain also became vulnerable to pressure to close the Burma Road, through which Chiang Kai-shek's armies were supplied. The British doubted that 'concessions from Burma on points of principle ... would bring any lasting improvement in Anglo-Japanese relations',[36] but agreed to suspend shipments for three months on the basis that any refusal would likely 'lead to war with Japan'.[37] Fraser reacted in no uncertain terms; his government had 'never believed, and we do not now believe' that:

> ...it was either wise or proper to attempt to placate Japan on the question of the Burma road ... The policy of 'appeasement' is in our view no more likely to be successful in the Far East than it was in Europe...[38]

The New Zealand War Cabinet considered the Asian situation so threatening that by August there was talk of holding the 3050 men of the Third Echelon — intended to build 2 NZ Division up to full strength — back in New Zealand.[39] Churchill wanted part of this force in Britain, and on 11 August, as the Luftwaffe struggled to smash the air defences over southeastern Britain, the Secretary of State for Dominion Affairs told Fraser that if, 'contrary to prudence and self-interest' the Japanese actually did surge into Sydney or Wellington, 'I have the explicit authority of Cabinet to assure you that we should then cut our losses in the Mediterranean and proceed to your aid, sacrificing every interest except only the defence of … this Island on which all depends.'[40] Churchill made the same assurance to Roosevelt, though he was concerned by the 'disastrous military possibilities' that would probably follow.[41]

Fraser then dropped his plan to send a delegation to Washington and suggested they might instead set up a diplomatic post. Churchill agreed. It was a longer process; preliminaries at the US end were not completed until December, and it was May 1941 before Fraser sent Gordon Coates and Frank Langstone to lay the groundwork. The legation was still formally unfilled in December when war broke out with Japan. These moves have been subject to a good deal of historical debate, invariably focusing on the degree to which Fraser's policy was an assertion of nationhood, and how that can be reconciled with New Zealand's ongoing loyalty to Britain.[42]

The fall of France also prompted developments within the Axis. An ascendant Germany was able to push closer ties with Japan, concluding the Tripartite Pact of September 1940, essentially a pragmatic extension of Bismarckian realpolitik. Hitler's Germany had almost nothing in common with Japan. The arrangement sent a message to the United States — though not, perhaps, as hawkish as sometimes considered. Konoe was prepared to accept strained relations as a price for economic independence, but did not want open conflict.[43]

Japanese forces advanced into French Indo-China that month, partly on the justification that it would cut off another Chinese supply route. International response was swift; Britain and the United States imposed sanctions on war materials and scrap iron. Relations cooled, and as Caldecote remarked to Fraser's government:

> While there is … an element of bluff in the Japanese attitude, and wiser elements in Japan cannot but be conscious of the adverse effects upon their economy of an extension of the policy of aggression, we cannot ignore the possibility that interventionists may before long gain complete control.[44]

Tensions between Japan and Britain were not helped by the Tripartite Pact, a point Churchill made to the Japanese ambassador in London during early 1940.[45] German foreign minister Joachim von Ribbentrop certainly pushed the Japanese to attack British possessions in the Far East.[46] From the perspective of the Konoe administration, however, the pact was of less import than the war in China, and the vulnerabilities that flowed from reliance on imported resources. Most of Japan's oil came from American and Dutch East Indies sources, and policy pushed during 1940 by the army called for the conquest of resource-rich areas in South East Asia as a quick road to economic self-sufficiency. Rather transparently, the proposed empire was called the Greater East Asia Co-Prosperity Sphere.[47] There was no immediate pressure to bring this to fruition, but in April 1941 Konoe's government concluded a five-year neutrality pact with Stalin, eliminating one variable from the political mix. The German attack on the Soviet Union three months later changed the ground rules again. Three strategies were available to Japan under this circumstance: attacking Thailand, attacking the Soviet Union, or securing the whole of Indo-China. Konoe's cabinet plumped for Indo-China, and on 21 July, Vichy French leader Admiral Darlan conceded to Japanese demands that they be permitted into Saigon.

The move was anticipated in the West and drew a sharp response. Roosevelt signed orders freezing Japanese assets, licensing Japanese imports into the United States and restricting oil exports to Japan.[48] Although Japan had reserves on hand, the loss of around 85 percent of its oil supply was decisive. Walter Nash summed it up in a hasty telegram to Fraser, then in London. 'It does not appear reasonably possible,' he warned. 'to avoid conflict with Japan if Indo-China is occupied.'[49] But it was not unexpected. Britain had asked New Zealand to bolster defences at Singapore as early as June. An RNZAF fighter squadron and construction crew were supplied — albeit with difficulty.[50]

The hawks of Konoe's cabinet did not take the prospect of slow strangulation lying down. A lobby group, including War Minister Tojo Hideki, favoured a military venture to get the Dutch East Indies oil supplies. Serious planning began in early August. These plans were not known to the British, but the general situation was nonetheless alarming, and plans floated by Admiralty staff during the latter half of 1941 called for a fleet deployment to Ceylon by early 1942, in numbers large enough to deter the Japanese, but not including the new battleships. Churchill disagreed, and by late October had persuaded the Admiralty to despatch the modern *Prince of Wales* and elderly battlecruiser *Repulse* to the Far East in advance of a larger fleet.[51] He advised Fraser.[52]

Tojo took effective control of the Japanese government in August, but the continued Japanese hold on Indo-China undermined diplomatic efforts to resolve the crisis, and preparations for an attack on the Kra Isthmus could not be entirely hidden. Churchill asked Roosevelt for a 'deterrent of the most general and formidable character'. The latter demurred, but Japan then offered a return to pre-July 1941 arrangements. In exchange they wanted oil. Roosevelt disagreed and on 26 November issued a 'Ten Point Note' which, as Churchill put it, 'not only met our wishes ... but indeed went beyond anything for which we had ventured to ask'.[53]

These demands — effectively a capitulate-or-fight ultimatum — fell on a Japanese cabinet in heroic mood. Only a few had doubts, notably Admiral Yamamoto Isoruku. Yet the facts were clear enough. Japan, with 14 percent of the world's industrial capacity, could not prevail long term against the Americans, who had nearly half, and where a gigantic military build-up was already under way. Japan could not match it, but to government officials in Tokyo a heavy enough blow delivered before the new US ships and aircraft began entering service in 1943–44 might make the Roosevelt administration think twice, perhaps even swing public opinion against a struggle.

This was the real point of miscalculation. Japanese leaders had all the facts about the United States, including details of the isolationist movement — but the reality of US society and culture was more than a list of empirical data, and American responses could not be interpreted by Japanese values. On 1 December Tojo resolved to attack the United States, Dutch East Indies and British Far Eastern possessions. Preparations were already well advanced: a force was ready to strike at the Kra Isthmus, and the striking force of the Combined Fleet was deep in the Pacific, waiting for orders to attack Pearl Harbor.

Neither Britain nor United States intelligence could locate the Japanese carriers. However, the force bearing down on the Kra Isthmus was clearly part of a thrust west. Early indications suggested the fleet was aimed at Thailand,[54] which prompted the British to consider forestalling the invasion by taking the Kra Isthmus themselves, or supporting the Thai government.[55] The invasion convoys were found by British reconnaissance aircraft on 6 December near Cambodia Point, and were seen to turn northwest, prompting speculation that they were heading for Bangkok.[56] The assault into Malaya came as a surprise on 8 December — 85 minutes before the air attack against Pearl Harbor on the other side of the date-line. Japan did not declare war prior to either assault.[57]

Main fleet to Singapore

Japanese plans were based on speed, surprise and — to some extent — good fortune. Tojo hoped to secure the co-prosperity sphere with a lightning 150-day campaign. The whole navy was available; but the 2.4 million-man army was heavily occupied in China, as was much of the army air force. Only 12 divisions and 700 aircraft were on hand for other purposes. Colonel Tsuji Manasobu, preparing plans to invade Malaya, calculated they would be outnumbered 2:1 on the ground. On the other hand, the 350,000 Allied troops in theatre were widely separated and poorly equipped, there was negligible naval opposition, and Allied air defences were no better off.

Forces committed to the Malayan campaign included the 60,000-strong 25th Army of General Yamashita Tomoyuki, backed by 459 army and 159 navy aircraft, and 80 tanks. To stop them, Lieutenant-General Arthur Percival had 85,000 troops and artillery, but just 150 aircraft, most of them obsolete. New Zealanders were in the front line — Kiwis in theatre included airmen woefully equipped with Brewster Buffaloes, but well-supported by New Zealand ground crews and engineers. Other Kiwis were serving on board the Royal Navy vessels in the area. Although determined to do their best, most of the defenders were poorly equipped, inadequately trained — largely because of the haste with which many had been deployed — and poorly served by their leaders. These factors were not likely to help morale, and there is some reason to believe that Percival was out of his depth — though most British commanders were still struggling to come to grips with modern warfare in 1941, a legacy of inter-war conservatism and a fixation on 1918 strategies.[58]

The two capital ships and destroyers, named Force Z, arrived in Singapore on 2 December, minus their intended aircraft carrier, and amid suggestions that they were being deployed too far forward. They were also only the vanguard; Phillips envisaged building the force up to four battleships and at least five cruisers, including *Achilles*, and basing it at Manila.[59] Japan could not attack such a fleet without over-weakening its position elsewhere in the Pacific. From New Zealand's perspective, however, Force Z assumed disproportionate value because, as Fraser reminded Churchill — the 'whole of this Dominion's defence preparations' were organised around the arrival of British naval forces at Singapore.[60] New Zealand's Chief of Naval Staff, Commodore W.E. Parry, was in Singapore as the Japanese attack began on 8 December and signalled the New Zealand Naval Board to send *Achilles* to reinforce them.

The Board agreed, and *Achilles* began a high-speed dash west. However, she had only got as far as Port Moresby before events rendered her journey pointless. Phillips decided to attack the invasion force at Singora. Force Z sailed late on the 8th, and was well into the Gulf of Siam before he was told there would be no air cover. He pressed on, which was not quite the rash decision it might seem in hindsight: at the time, the British were unaware of the extent to which the Japanese had developed air attack at sea, nor of the range of the Japanese bombers, nor that the specialist anti-shipping squadrons were already in Saigon. In any event, the Royal Navy had been operating under conditions of enemy air superiority in European waters for some time, without calamity to any of its capital ships. While Phillips was later criticised for taking such action, in any case, with ships that had been intended to form a 'fleet in being', Royal Navy tradition was always to engage the enemy and, in surface action, Force Z had adequate fire-power against likely convoy escorts, such as several of the Japanese heavy cruisers, or their rebuilt First World War vintage battlecruisers.

Unfortunately the British did not find the Japanese invasion forces that day. Phillips decided to abandon the mission next day, and then at midnight heard that the Japanese were landing at Kuantan. He changed course to investigate, found the harbour empty early on the 10th, and set course for Singapore. The squadron was around 170 miles northeast of the city late next morning when it was located by a Japanese reconnaissance aircraft, which directed 88 Mitsubishi G4M1 'Betty' and Nakajima G3M3 'Nell' torpedo-bombers of the 22nd Air Flotilla to the attack.

The assault began at 11.10 am and was initially pressed home by eight bombers, named the Genzan group after their flight-leader, five of which were damaged by the 5.25-inch DP armament of the *Prince of Wales*. Smaller weapons joined in as the aircraft approached. 'Our "Chicago pianos" (multiple pom-poms) open up, all our triple ... high-angle turrets ... The uproar is tremendous,' a survivor from *Repulse* recalled.[61] The Japanese scored one hit on *Repulse*. Half an hour later the ships came under attack from the Mihoro and Kanoya groups of 25 aircraft. Nine attacked the *Prince of Wales* with Type 91 torpedoes. These had 330-lb (165-kg) hexyl charges, within the design parameters of the battleship's underwater protective system. However, she was also struck the port side aft at the weakest point of the system, just above the propeller shafts; and this proved disastrous. A hole some 24 by 15 feet (8 x 5 m) was blown in the shell plating, the void spaces between frames 184 and 253 flooded, the port propeller shaft was bent, and water gushed into 'B' engine room along the shaft alley. Efforts to pump the space clear were unsuccessful and Lieutenant D.B.H. Wildish, the officer in charge, ordered the compartment abandoned.

Another torpedo then caused a bulkhead between two main watertight compartments to fail, and the men in the port cypher room and port aft 5.25-

inch magazines evacuated them without closing the watertight doors. Within ten minutes, the ship had a list of 11.5 degrees to port, a stern trim of three feet, and was reduced to 16 knots. Damage control parties established flooding boundaries around 12.20 pm, but five of the eight turbo-generators were inoperative, preventing the after 5.25-inch guns from firing and immobilising half the main pumps. The system could normally handle up to 8900 tons of water an hour.

The remaining torpedo-bombers attacked *Repulse*. Captain W.G. Tennant handled the old battlecruiser with remarkable verve, turning at high speed to 'comb' the tracks. At 12.26 pm, 26 torpedo-bombers attacked both ships, scoring one hit on *Repulse*. A few minutes later nine more torpedo-bombers hurtled in from several directions, scoring a hit that jammed her steering gear. Three more hits followed, and *Repulse* began heeling rapidly. She sank at 12.33 pm with the loss of 513 officers and men.[62]

During the same attack *Prince of Wales* was torpedoed once amidships, then twice more aft on the starboard side. Eight aircraft bombed her at 12.41 pm, scoring one hit; but the near-misses were apparently more crucial because they damaged the side plating and increased the inflow of water. By this time the battleship had 18,000 tons of water on board, and her stability was threatened by free-surface effects. She was clearly going down. The destroyer *Electra* came alongside to take off her crew, and at 1.15 pm the *Prince of Wales* suddenly rolled to port, capsizing five minutes later in a flurry that almost took down *Electra*. Some 870 men were lost on both ships, including New Zealanders Reverend W.G. Parker and Joiner K.H.W. Morgan.[63] Kiwi pilot Lieutenant (A) G.M. Holden was airborne in *Repulse*'s Walrus when the attack occurred and landed the amphibian in open ocean, where he was rescued by an RNZAF-manned Catalina.[64]

The ships were within range of Singapore based fighters, but the alarm was not raised until *Repulse* signalled that the squadron was under attack. Even then, the RNZAF's 488 Squadron pilots were simply told to fly in pairs at half-hour intervals to a given location. By the time the first arrived, Force Z was on the bottom.[65] Just over 2000 survivors returned to Singapore, jammed like sardines on the destroyers.

The loss to Britain was proportionately greater than US losses at Pearl Harbor; and for New Zealand the defeat of Force Z was — as the *New Zealand Herald* put it — a matter of 'deep gravity', a moral blow well out of proportion to the sinking of two ships.[66] Singapore had loomed large in New Zealand strategic thinking for 20 years. The base had been built in part with New

Zealand money at the expense of local defences at home. While Singapore remained intact, and while a mobile British fleet was based either there or in the vicinity, Japan could not extend itself southeast to strike New Zealand. Now all that had changed.

The fall of Singapore

Dr Goebbels at his worst has seldom been more puerile or dishonest than British officialdom in its versions of what is happening in Malaya
— The Press, 5 January 1942.[67]

Yamashita's forces met only marginal opposition in the Thai ports of Singora and Patani. Brigadier B.W. Key organised an effective defence of Kota Bahru, but this did not reduce the impact of landings further up the coast, and Yamashita's men began a relentless advance south. Jitra was taken on 12 December. The 25th Army overran Penang on 16 December, capturing stocks abandoned by the retreating British.

Allied response was slowed by lack of naval and air power, and in mid-December Fraser made the obvious point to Churchill: 'The defeat of Japan is essentially a question of sea power ... To attain this ... it is essential that all naval forces in the Pacific Ocean ... should be under one unified command.'[68] This was indeed what the Allies had in mind, and a combined American, British, Dutch and Australian command (ABDA) was set up a few weeks later under General Sir Archibald Wavell. But it did not include New Zealand, nor bring all available forces under Wavell's wing.

Wavell visited the Malaya front mid-January to discover that the Japanese had won a decisive victory on the Slim River. The 'two forward brigades were reduced to a handful of very tired men'.[69] He urged Percival to stiffen the forces on the Johore side of the peninsula, and was 'concerned to find' that there were no defences 'on the north side of Singapore island'.[70] The other problem was lack of air support, and Wavell planned to hold a line from Darwin to Timor, Java and Singapore, 'on which to build up ... an air force capable of securing local air superiority and thereby checking the Japanese advance southwards'.[71] A 'formidable' force of 1000 US aircraft was expected to arrive 'within the next two or three months', but as Wavell observed, 'even had all the aircraft arrived, we should have had considerable difficulty in finding sufficient aerodrome accommodation and ground organisation'.[72]

New Zealanders were in the thick of the defence, both in the air and at sea; some 32 officers and men had been sent to Singapore under 'Scheme Y' to man motor launches on the Malayan coast. The boats were soon in action, 'chased by the Jap planes from one end of Malaya to the other', as Lieutenant Geoffry Inns put it in a letter home:

> *At one stage we were sitting on a river in No Man's Land with our artillery firing over us and the Jap mortars banging back … and their aeroplanes looking for us at heights of 50 feet, but we are camouflage experts now and they couldn't find us. We have taken part in shellings and sinkings round the Jap-held coast with them firing star shells looking for us. We have been on evacuations and raiding parties and Lord knows what else.*[73]

The Japanese pushed south, and Wavell was horrified to discover that preparations to defend Singapore Island had still to be completed. Efforts to stop the advance at Bakri and Parit Sulong failed, and at the beginning of February Singapore became a fortress under siege. In theory the place had been set up for the purpose. but in fact defence was no better organised than in Malaya. The material Percival needed — including 50 Hurricanes — arrived late, and most was destroyed by air attack before it could be unloaded.[74] However, Percival also failed to follow Wavell's instruction to build defences along the north of the island, and implemented no measures to protect civilians — this on the logic that it would be bad for morale.[75]

Only a handful of fighters were left by this time, and the vulnerability of airfields to shellfire from Malaya restricted operations to Kallang. The RNZAF construction crew worked to fill in craters. 'Repairs were made by throwing into craters any large rocks, rubble etc which were to hand', Flight Lieutenant P.L. Laing reported later.[76] The Japanese — ironically operating from RNZAF-built airfields in southern Malaya — dominated the skies.

Percival still had 18 Division and 8 Australian Division to hand, along with the 15-inch naval guns in the fortress at Changi. However, although the weapons could be swivelled to face Malaya, spotting was a problem and the guns were optimised for sea targets. The outcome seemed inevitable, and the pause while Yamashita's men assembled on the north side of the Johore strait gave an opportunity to pull out civilians and non-essential personnel. A detachment of New Zealand engineers left for Batavia on board HMS *Kedah* on 31 January. Next day the RNZAF's Aerodrome Construction Squadron began loading their equipment on board the *Talthybius*, but she was sunk by an air raid.⁷⁷ The end seemed close, and opinion in Whitehall was realistic about it: 'we no longer nursed illusions about the protracted defence of Singapore',⁷⁸ and the Chiefs of Staff were already contemplating a 'scorched earth' policy. The possibility of Japan taking — and using — Britain's largest naval base outside European waters was unthinkable. On 2 February Churchill urged that the 'docks and workshops ... [be] rendered utterly useless for at least eighteen months'.⁷⁹

Three of Singapore's four airfields then came under artillery attack, and Wavell made the decision to withdraw the fighters to Sumatra.⁸⁰ By this time Japanese aircraft were roaming over and beyond Singapore, looking for targets of opportunity. The New Zealanders were ordered to leave on the *City of Canterbury* and coaster *Darvel*. The *City of Canterbury* sailed on the night of the 6th, but *Darvel* was recalled because she was too slow, and an attempt next day was aborted by bad weather. She finally sailed on the 8th. Her captain hoped to run the Banka Strait at night, but they were delayed two hours assisting the *Kiritak*, and anchored near an abandoned steamer in the hope of hiding from Japanese patrols. They were found anyway, and twenty-seven bombers launched an attack late next morning:

> *There was a minute or two of suspense as the drone of many aircraft engines grew louder... then came the rush and whistle of falling bombs, and hell seemed let loose in a pandemonium of noise. Terrific explosions shook the ship. She tossed and rolled like a cork as bombs exploded and churned the water all round. Columns of spray shot up and drenched those flattened out on the decks. There was a hiss of steam from burst pipes and clatter of falling debris. The bombs stopped falling. A burst or two of machine gun fire, then all was quiet.*⁸¹

Another raid swept overhead five minutes later, sinking the abandoned ship and leaving the *Darvel* riddled. The lifeboats were damaged and 'it was decided to weigh anchor and drive the ship all out for Java'.⁸² The RNZAF engineers plugged the holes,⁸³ and *Darvel* limped into Batavia on 12 February.

Yamashita's forces crossed the Johore Strait on the night of 8–9 February. Wavell ordered Percival to launch a counter-attack, but had no real 'confidence in any prolonged resistance'.⁸⁴ On the 11th the ground crews of 488 Squadron were evacuated on board the *Empire Star*, which came under air attack as they left the docks. Next morning they were attacked at sea and put up stiff resistance with machine guns and rifles, shooting down one aircraft and damaging another.

New Zealand born Able Seaman L.C. Hurndell, on board the gunboat *Grasshopper*, realised something was up when the Japanese raided the city on the night of 8 December; and by the 12th the tiny ship was working with two troop transports to evacuate survivors:

> We were standing off... about 5–6 miles out and we could see the dive-bombers just machine gunning and dive bombing around the city. There was no air opposition at all and it was just chaotic. The fires were burning and all the oil tanks were burning and Singapore was just a massive glow at night... we finally went in about 11 pm on the night of the 12th to Clifford Pier to take out the last of the survivors. The Japanese by that time were just down the road about half a mile away... We were subjected to a mortar attack and mortar shells were exploding all around us, but funnily enough not one hit us. Whether it was our good luck or poor aiming by the Japs, I'll never know.[85]

Percival, inside his underground command bunker on Canning Hill — the 'Battle Box' — delayed giving up the fight; but counter-attacks proved fruitless and once the Seletar reservoirs had been taken the end was inevitable. Without water, the city could not survive more than a few days. He reluctantly surrendered to Yamashita on the 15th. A few ships were still able to get away. *Grasshopper* picked up a mixed batch of civilians, servicemen and a handful of Japanese prisoners, and sailed at midnight for Java with *Dragonfly* and a motor launch. They did not get far; late next morning Japanese aircraft sank *Dragonfly* and 'blew the middle' out of *Grasshopper*, wounding Hurndell. The survivors jumped into the water, but:

> ...the Japs came down machine gunning us and as they went away the rear gunner would have a go and they killed a hell of a lot of people in the water.... We lost most of the civilians and we lost most of the children, they were killed on the mess deck ... [when] the bomb exploded ... I managed to get ashore somehow ... I remember being placed on native matting and being put under a native house or hut on poles while waiting to be evacuated ... I eventually finished up on an island called Singkep ... we eventually became prisoners of war...[86]

In all, about 80 small ships tried to leave Singapore. Almost all were sunk. One of the survivors — another New Zealander — took to a small boat and, 'after many adventures', reached Batavia, though that was only temporary refuge in the face of the Japanese advance.[87]

Samurai blitzkrieg

The Japanese ground attack on Malaya and Singapore was only the first part of a substantial assault by Japanese forces on the whole of South East Asia, essentially to secure the rubber and other resources of the region along with the flanks of what was euphemistically dubbed the 'co-prosperity sphere'. Much of the area was either held by the British, or represented British interests, but although the Japanese threat had been long recognised, the scale of forces available to defend it was minimal.

This masked the fact that Japanese ground forces were not immense by European standards, and they lacked heavy tanks. But they had almost total air superiority and were pushing into thin opposition. Hong Kong fell in a confused surrender over Christmas and Boxing days 1941, while armies in Thailand advanced to attack Burma — a 'most important but somewhat distracting commitment' as far as Wavell was concerned.[88] Defences there comprised a collection of British and Indian units under Lieutenant-General Sir William Slim. General Claire Chennault sent three squadrons of 'Flying Tigers' — a volunteer US air force operating in China — but there were not enough of them.[89] By February 1942 the Japanese 32 Division was approaching Rangoon, and Slim's meagre forces had to retreat to India.[90]

United States' interests also came under direct attack. General Homma Masaharu's 14th Army attacked the Philippines on 10 December. Defence was co-ordinated by US General Douglas MacArthur, who overestimated the abilities of the poorly trained Filipino troops at his disposal. Within a fortnight the Japanese had taken Luzon, Mindanao and Jolo and were preparing a major advance on Manila from two directions. MacArthur declared Manila an open city and withdrew to the Bataan Peninsula. Fighting continued for four months. MacArthur was ordered to leave in early March, and US forces in the Philippines surrendered on 9 April. Only Corrigedor stood, but its reduction was only a matter of time, and General Jonathan Wainwright surrendered the fortress in early May.[91]

The Japanese then advanced deep into the Pacific to deflect the expected US counter-attack. They had a head start; the Marshall, Caroline and Marianas islands — with the exception of US-held Guam — were Japanese protectorates. Guam had never been fortified and fell in half an hour, the day after the Pearl Harbour attack. Wake Island followed, along with Nauru and Ocean Islands and their vital phosphate deposits. A strike southeast in late January took New Ireland and the vital deep-water harbour at Rabaul on the northern tip of New Britain.

The attack on the Dutch East Indies — the real target of the whole operation — began in mid-January 1942 with assaults on Tarakan and Manado. By early February, the Japanese had advanced through Balikpapan, Kendari, Ambon and Ulin, and on 9 February they took Makassar. Java was next. Wavell warned the Chiefs of Staff that its defence was 'extremely doubtful' and recommended diverting the Australia Corps — which were being brought home from the Middle East — to Burma. It did no good; he was told to defend Java to the last man.[92] A scratch Allied cruiser force tried to stop the invasion fleet, but was defeated on 27 February, and Wavell recommended disbanding the ABDA. The government of the Dutch East Indies surrendered on 8 March. These victories gave Japan the oil resources it needed, albeit via a slender sea route. They also gained a stranglehold over world rubber supplies, 90 percent of which came from Malaya.

Allied forces, New Zealanders among them, hastened to escape as Japan advanced through Java. Most of the 'Scheme Y' force had taken their motor launches to Batavia when Singapore fell, abandoning these to board the minesweeper HMS *Wokwang* on 3 March. They shaped course for Australia, but were intercepted by a Japanese destroyer force. *Wokwang* was sunk, and although 18 survivors took to a life-raft, only two survived a three-week ordeal at sea and a difficult landing.[93]

Japan still had to secure the southeastern perimeter of its new empire, and planned to do so by taking Port Moresby and pushing east to take the Solomons, Fiji and Samoa. Air and sea forces in Port Moresby could dominate the Coral Sea while air units further east could simultaneously throttle the trans-Pacific supply lines to Australasia and reduce the risk of the US using the southern continent as a base. The Imperial Japanese Navy actually recommended invading Australia, but the army had heavy Asian commitments and could not spare the dozen divisions thought necessary.[94] Air attacks nonetheless began on Darwin in mid-February. Meanwhile the South Seas Force advanced southeast from Rabaul into the Solomons, landing on Bougainville at the end of March. Japan, it seemed, was now on New Zealand's front doorstep.

CHAPTER TWO

Desperate Defence

You will understand that a handful of Hudsons reinforced by numerous obsolete bombers and trainers will make an impression more for gallantry than for their execution...
— Peter Fraser to British Prime Minister Winston Churchill, 19 February 1942[1]

The Japanese attack into the Pacific brought to reality a nightmare that the New Zealand government and people had been expecting since 1904. Popular fears portrayed Japanese transports disgorging a rampaging horde into Queen Street or Aotea Quay. Such thinking was exaggerated, but New Zealand certainly faced several threats during the early months of 1942, notably isolation and, with it, starvation. Before the war, Labour radical John A. Lee had argued that isolation would 'dislocate our economy' but 'not afflict us with hunger'.[2] In fact New Zealand had mechanised with alacrity, and by 1940 the country relied on imported petrol, lubricants, rubber and machinery to run the industries, farms, orchards, market gardens and transport networks. If New Zealand was cut off then hunger — especially in the urban centres — would almost certainly follow. An official US assessment in March 1942 opined that New Zealand's isolation 'will probably be sufficient for ... [Japanese] purposes'.[3]

Such a fate seemed near by late 1941. There were already shortages of fuel and industrial goods as a downstream effect of the European war, and German raiding vessels had shown that trans-Tasman trade and even the crucial inter-island connections could be threatened by a resolute enemy. War with Japan compounded all these issues. Government responded promptly; fuel was more sharply rationed and even rail travel was limited to 100-mile (160-km) journeys, with no guarantee that return travel would be possible. Some people panicked, 'besieging petrol service stations' in an 'attempt to exchange whatever December and January coupons they held for precious benzine'.[4] Government reacted by initially withdrawing some coupons,[5] and on 15 December banning petrol sales altogether in an effort to prevent stocks running dry.[6] Fuel for commercial vehicles was still available, but some local authorities went further, as in Christchurch where bread deliveries were cancelled as a 'means of conserving petrol and manpower'.[7]

Submarines in the South Pacific

Fears of blockade had a practical edge to them. Japan conducted a small but sustained submarine campaign into the South Pacific through the first year of the war — ten 'I' boats patrolled as far as Zanzibar, the South Pacific and western coast of the United States.[8] I-20 was despatched to the South Pacific in November, and was off Fiji in January. She was found by the auxiliary cruiser HMNZS *Monowai*, which was escorting the passenger vessel *Taroona* back to Auckland after dropping off reinforcements for 8 New Zealand Brigade. The little convoy had just left Suva on the afternoon of 16 January, and was zigzagging as an anti-submarine precaution when two 'heavy explosions' sent water and black smoke rocketing into the air nearby. Captain G.R. Deverell ordered action stations and began snaking, while lookouts searched for what was thought to be an aircraft. Able Seaman Malcolm Mackay spotted a conning tower. Deverell ordered the 6 and 3-inch guns to open fire, then altered course to comb any torpedo tracks — a mistake, as the guns only fired a few rounds before they could no longer bear. In those moments *Monowai* straddled the submarine and Deverell saw 'two shorts that appeared to be very close'.[9]

One crew member recalled the consternation that followed. 'I can hear old Paddy Bourke ... the Gunnery Officer, screaming his head off from the Gunnery Control Tower above us, for the Captain to open the A Arcs.'[10] The submarine lobbed five rounds at the New Zealand vessel before crash-diving. On board *Monowai* the bridge crew 'finally heeded old Paddy's screaming' and the auxiliary cruiser turned back again, firing 11 rounds of 6-inch and 12 of 3-inch at the submarine as it disappeared. The shooting was 'absolutely superb', one sailor recalled later. 'When you realise there was no radar in those days, we only had a range-finder up top.'[11]

Deverell ordered *Taroona* to 'return through the Mbennga passage' and led the way with *Monowai*. The tide was up and the 'dangerous Caesar rocks' were invisible, but navigating officer Lieutenant G.H. Edwards got them through safely. Deverell later praised Edwards' efforts and added that the engines 'rose to the occasion excellently and in spite of leaky boilers and condensers, and defective turbo-generators, a speed of 95 revolutions (nominally 18.1 knots) was quickly reached'.[12]

Other Japanese boats ranged as far as New Zealand waters. I-29 apparently entered Cook Strait in February 1942, looking for troop transports. The submarine surfaced with impunity off the capital and Pilot Fujita Nobuo reconnoitred Port Nicholson with the float-plane, finding 'four or five' merchants in harbour. A little later, I-29's crew spotted the inter-island ferry, but orders explicitly prohibited an attack. I-25 arrived in the South Pacific during March, encountering the armed merchant *Tongariro* en route from Fremantle to Wellington. The Japanese boat went on to Cook Strait and made a further reconnaissance flight over the capital, then coasted north to the Hauraki Gulf apparently unseen — though the minesweeper HMNZS *Viti* reported a dubious hydrophone detection.

I-21 made a similar sortie in May, via Fiji. This time the target was Auckland. The boat surfaced off Mayor Island in the Bay of Plenty, and Lieutenant Isumo Ito took a float-plane across Thames. Low cloud and rain hampered his effort, but he 'circled Auckland at about 1200 feet and observed some small boats which he thought were fishing craft lying in the harbour'. The submarine was meant to head to Wellington, but the mission was abandoned when news came that a simultaneous midget submarine attack into Sydney Harbour had failed.[13]

The ease with which these manoeuvres were conducted was a telling indictment of New Zealand's vulnerability, and the attack on Sydney prompted precautions against similar raids into New Zealand harbours. Blackout was extended to coastal street lights and towns, thrusting many places into what the Evening Post classified as 'Stygian gloom'.[14] There were more reports of submarines in New Zealand waters during June, and although the Solomons campaign of late 1942 diverted Japanese attentions there, the I-boats were back in the Tasman by early 1943, preying mostly on Australian coastal shipping. One passed through Cook Strait in February.[15]

Invasion was a separate matter. Australia was the obvious target in early 1942. The British Chiefs of Staff considered that Japan might deploy only a brigade group beyond, but this was dismissed as 'fantastic' in New Zealand. The Chief of General Staff, Lieutenant-General Edward Puttick, thought a range of scenarios more likely.¹⁶ If Allied naval forces were available, attack would 'consist of sporadic raids only'. In their absence, division-strength forces backed by four aircraft carriers and a second division was 'possible', and he felt that capture of Fiji or New Caledonia was not a pre-condition.¹⁷ Cabinet concurred, and Fraser warned Churchill that the British 'brigade group' idea was an 'attempt to think in terms of the past'. He added: 'if this line of thought is persisted in we must brace ourselves to meet the fate of Malaya and with infinitely less reason or excuse'.¹⁸

Defending New Zealand 1940–42

> *'…to-night we are facing dangers such as we have never known in these islands … at this critical hour we must face the future with good heart and deep determination to do all and give all in the struggle for our country…'*
> — New Zealand Prime Minister Peter Fraser, 8 March 1942¹⁹

In mid-March 1942, Auckland Mayor and local Emergency Precautions Service chairman J.A.C. Allum presided over an agitated public meeting. Government, he felt, had not taken adequate steps to evacuate Auckland if invasion loomed, and he feared that 'women and children' might have to be 'moved amid all the difficulties of a state of emergency'.²⁰ His sentiments highlighted popular feeling, and in many respects the sense of crisis that struck New Zealand during early 1942 was unsurprising. The North African campaign was entering a critical phase — 2 NZ Division had just saved the 8th Army from defeat outside Tobruk, at heavy cost, and long casualty lists appeared in local papers during December, alongside news of Japanese successes in the Pacific.²¹ Even censorship could not disguise the gloom. Dire warnings of 'Critical times', 'Full War Footing' and 'Call to Service'²² were joined by other, nastier alarms: 'Rangoon in flames', 'Java battle, Bandoeng's fall', and 'Australian fears', among others.²³ Reports that the Australian government had authorised a 'scorched earth' policy did not lift the mood.²⁴ Cartoonists dropped jovialities. 'Time is short,' Gordon Minhinnick wrote beneath an evocative image of soldiers and civilians hoisting an unexploded bomb away from 'Your Home'.²⁵

In fact New Zealand was not as vulnerable as public fears suggested. The forward defensive policy laid out during the 1939 Pacific Defence Conference had been largely implemented by early 1942 — within the limits of equipment shortages. In theory, New Zealand naval and air forces based in Fiji could search a wide arc, finding any raiding forces or supply ships on their way in. The islands straddled the communications lines south and had to be taken before Japan could mount a successful invasion of New Zealand. By late 1941, Fiji's own army was being developed to brigade strength. The New Zealand 8th Brigade Group was also deployed there along with all New Zealand's heavy anti-aircraft weaponry — four Bofors cannons — and three of the four available radar sets.[26] These DSIR-built units were designed for air-detection, and in the event proved capable of also tracking seaborne targets, including surfaced Japanese submarines.[27]

These were significant forces, but the whole scheme still relied on air power, and the teeth had been drawn by the 1939 decision to hand the RNZAF's 30 Wellington bombers over to the RAF.[28] The only long-range aircraft in New Zealand by 1940 were two TEAL passenger flying boats and a handful of land-based airliners.[29] Most were impressed for training and patrol work. The TEAL boats continued to serve the essential trans-Tasman link but were on call for military use — running at least 16 reconnaissance operations between mid-1940 and early 1942.[30] The de Havilland airliners were sent to Fiji and were joined, towards the end of 1941, by three obsolete Short Singapore III flying boats, operating from Lauthala Bay.[31] They did not have much offensive power, and loading bombs into the TEAL boats — as was actually tried at least once — was not an answer. German merchant raiders operated around New Zealand waters during 1940 with virtual impunity. Fraser's effort to get Hudson patrol bombers highlighted the problem. He argued to Churchill in December that:

> *We have constantly borne in mind the necessity of taking a large view and of balancing our needs with those elsewhere in the common cause, but we wonder if it is fully realised in the United Kingdom how helpless this Dominion is against attacks from seaward. As you know, the whole of our defence measures were built on the assurance that in time of potential trouble in these waters adequate naval forces would be available. They are not ... We believe we are the only Dominion in this situation, and we are reminded every day that we would not have been in this situation had we not, voluntarily and unasked, decided to release the Wellingtons...*[32]

The focus shifted during 1941 to home defence. Early in the year, government invited General Sir Guy Williams to New Zealand to help develop anti-invasion precautions. His recommendations included a range of harbour-defence booms and minefields, particularly around Auckland. The Pacific war began before anything could be done, but in late December the government decided to lay the proposed Auckland minefields as soon as feasible. Mines were in short supply, but after a vigorous dispute over the advantages of deploying them around New Caledonia, 200 were finally laid off Auckland by HMAS Bungaree in March.[33] Other minefields followed later in the year.

Direct defence drew attention in August 1941, when the war cabinet decided to train the New Zealand Home Defence Forces 'to the standard of overseas troops'. This was partly to provide better reinforcements for 2 NZ Division in Egypt, but also to produce a 'more adequately trained and organised body for the defence of the Dominion'. Nash gave Churchill a shopping list that included 38,000 rifles and bayonets, 582 anti-tank guns, 2500 Bren guns, and 170 M3 light tanks.[34] Some had been released to New Zealand when Nash made the request, and more was to hand — including the first of the Hudsons — when war broke out with Japan, providing a good range of equipment for direct defence. But there was still not enough, and without a fighter arm the country remained vulnerable. J.G. Coates, in the United States to lay the groundwork for the diplomatic legation, discussed war material without success.

Civil defence was handled by the Emergency Precautions Service, organised at local body level, which arranged everything from road-sign removal to air-raid precautions, fire-fighting, and even such mundane matters as scrap recovery.[35] The scheme had actually emerged from the 1931 Hawke's Bay earthquake, when ad hoc emergency arrangements worked well, but a more formal set-up was clearly needed. The basic structures were in place by 1939.[36] Local politics occasionally intruded, but in general the scheme met the need.[37] Blackouts were formally introduced towards the end of 1941 despite public grumbling.[38] These were strictly enforced — Christchurch EPS wardens went so far as to cut off power 'for one week in the first instance and one month for a second offence'.[39]

War with Japan prompted further action. In January 1942 the government ordered full mobilisation. This arrangement between state and private enterprise harnessed the whole capacity of New Zealand's population of around 1.7 million to the war effort, including the total direction of labour, by order, to wherever it was needed — civil or military. By this time some 27,000 men were in training, many for a new armoured brigade which, after much soul-searching, government decided to retain in New Zealand. A total of around 50,000 men were under arms in the country, divided into 23 battalions. A further 18 battalions, nine rifle regiments and four field regiments were in formation. Some 17,500 men — including married men with children —

were called up in March. Newspapers warned men to 'place their private and business affairs in order immediately'.[40]

To these forces could be added the 26,500 men ballotted to join the Territorials, and the 100,000 men of the Home Guard, although the latter were not well armed.[41] Put another way, the total number of Kiwis in the forces — including the 61,368 overseas, but not the Home Guard — amounted to '…7.6 percent of the total population and 38 percent of the men within the age groups from which they were drawn'.[42] Heavy weaponry by this time included several batteries of 6-inch guns, 36 25-pounders and 50 18-pounders.[43] These numbers were well in excess of what estimates suggested Japan could field into New Zealand, and explains why there was no government clamour for the return of forces serving in the Middle East. Former Labour MP John A. Lee wanted a brigade pulled back, but his was a lone voice.[44]

However, none of this was likely to count for much in the absence of fighter aircraft. As Fraser remarked, 'the success of anti-invasion operations depends to the greatest extent on air superiority, without which our land forces and coast defences will be at the worst possible disadvantage'.[45] In early 1942, some 108 de Havilland DH 82 Tiger Moth biplane trainers were nominated for combat duties under emergency plans.[46] This was pure desperation; and Fraser put the issue to Churchill:

> …*no reasonable security against carrier-borne air attack can be provided unless the limited air striking forces available are provided with fighter protection. In addition [we] … consider that some fighter protection in the form of interceptor aircraft is essential for the protection of at least the two main ports of Auckland and Wellington…*[47]

Churchill demurred; Britain could provide just 18 modern fighters.[48] An alarmed Fraser protested. New Zealand needed 36 to meet training obligations for the RAF alone, plus another four squadrons against the Japanese threat.[49] However, Britain was in no position to do much other than promise to 'do our best to help in consultation with the Americans'.[50]

Invasion 1942 — myth and reality

Although New Zealanders popularly feared a Japanese invasion in 1942, and government took the issue seriously enough to engage in preparations, as far as could be managed, official military opinion suggested that this was the least likely of the practical threats that war with Japan posed to New Zealand. Nor could it come without warning: Fiji had to be taken before operations further south could be sustained, and the British thought Japan would deploy only a brigade to New Zealand at most. US staff planners initially even doubted that, suggesting blockade as a more likely strategy.[51]

New Zealand escaped both fates, but it turned out that the threat was no chimera. New Zealand — along with Australia — featured in all incarnations of Japan's Co-Prosperity Sphere as it evolved during 1940. Most versions incorporated the two Dominions as part of the 'inner sphere' considered vital to Japanese economic interests. This was reflected in arrangements Japanese diplomats reached with Germany and Italy during July 1940, when Japanese Foreign office officials concluded that the 'New Order in the Far East' should 'extend from Burma and the eastern part of India to New Zealand'.[52]

This meant direct invasion;[53] and the occupation plan for New Zealand, in anticipation of an invasion plan itself, was drafted in detail by the Kokusaku Kenkyu Kai (National Policy Research Institute) to the point of discussing the geographical limits of a 'New Zealand Government-General' and nominating an administrator.[54] Full details of the occupation plan were not finalised, but the available details were obtained by the New Zealand government in 1947, and it appeared that the country would certainly have faced a bleak future if an invasion had succeeded.

Initial administration would probably have been similar to that of other occupied British territories such as Singapore, which was operated as a military dictatorship in which non-Japanese were second-rate citizens. Longer term, Japanese planners envisaged limited self-rule, framed within the total subjugation of New Zealand's economy and foreign policy to Japanese needs, all under the control of a single powerful officer who reported to Tokyo. In particular, key state assets and infrastructure such as the power system, railways, telephone system and so forth would have been passed as monopolies into foreign private hands — the Japanese industrial *zaibatsu* — at peppercorn sale prices, then the profits from them siphoned into those Japanese hands. Meanwhile, New Zealand's pastoral production was to be sold to Japan, again at ruinous rates; and the country would also have been used as a dumping ground for surplus industrial products, such as cars, sold into the economy at a profit to the manufacturers.[55]

It was classic economic imperialism; and while no responsible government would do this to its own people, a conquering power easily had the ability to enforce such policies. Although the specifics of the planned Japanese occupation were not known in 1942, the thrust of how such things might pan out was certainly familiar to the government. And that was quite apart from the other suffering that occupation would bring.

However, there was a difference between plans to occupy and the practical realities of staging and supporting an invasion force that far into the South Pacific. The rapid expansion into South East Asia and the western Pacific had been conducted with relatively minimal forces; and Japanese planners knew that military advances beyond the initial objectives of the 150-day blitzkrieg would depend heavily on the course of events. Possible follow-on strategies were discussed in Japanese command circles during early 1942, and US investigators were told after the war that, Japan had indeed 'contemplated' operations 'in the Fiji, New Zealand, Samoa and New Caledonia areas'.[56] These, however, were intended to isolate Australasia from US support and reinforce the Japanese position in the Pacific, not to invade New Zealand or even Australia.

From a strategic perspective such a move was sensible and, indeed, necessary if Japan was to hold what it had taken against the inevitable counter-attacks, and concrete planning got as far as a scheme to take the Fiji-Samoa line, which was intended to follow the operations against Port Moresby and Midway. In mid-May 1942 the 17th Army was established under Lieutenant-General Hyakutake Haruyoshi for the purpose, with an expected assault date in July.

In the event, the thrusts against Port Moresby and Midway failed, and the island-chain advance got only as far as the Solomons.[57] Had Japan not suffered these reverses, attacks on New Caledonia, Fiji and Samoa would have taken place, and New Zealand would have been cut off by August 1942 at the latest; and Japanese forces would have had the capacity to interdict efforts to supply certainly New Zealand, and potentially eastern Australia. Historic counter-factuals are always speculative, but it seems clear that if the US had lost the remaining aircraft carriers of the Pacific Fleet at Midway, any further intervention would have had to wait until the new ships under construction had been completed and assembled into a useful force, probably towards the end of 1943 at the earliest.[58]

If this had happened, New Zealand's outlook would have been bleak. Local agricultural and pastoral production had long since been motorised by the early 1940s, as had the main transport networks. As the Japanese experience demonstrated when their own home islands were blockaded in 1944–45, severe fuel shortages, leading to breakdown of transport networks, urban depopulation and disease would all have been major issues within a few months, irrespective of the resolution of government and people. Even as matters stood, with the sea lanes open, By early 1942, 'gas producers' developed by the DSIR were available to bolt on to vehicles and run them with coal and wood; but neither fuel was a real substitute for oil, particularly as New Zealand only just mined enough coal for its own peacetime uses at the time. It is unlikely that New Zealand government and society would have collapsed; but life would have been unpleasant and the war effort reduced to negligible value.

Whether Japan would have invaded New Zealand after taking the Fiji-Samoa line was unlikely in practise, given the limits of Japan's military capacity. Nor was it really necessary: merely taking the South Pacific island chains, alone, would have slashed New Zealand's support lines – forcing any imports to be run around southern routes at reduced scale in consequence of the distance, and probably averting any need for a militarily expensive invasion. As the Americans discovered later, operations were certainly 'contemplated', but opinion within Japanese military circles was not unanimous, and — as the split attack on the Solomons and Midway reveals — often marked by compromise between inconsistent goals. A thrust south would have competed with Rear-Admiral Ugaki Matome's scheme to push north and take Hawaii.[59]

Even if the assault on New Zealand had been launched, its outcome is also speculative. The question is whether the numerical advantage and personal resolve of the defending forces, operating on home ground, could have offset total Japanese air superiority and the effects of problems consequent on New Zealand's isolation. However, the fact remains that none of this was known in 1942 as the crisis unfolded – when the unknowns of Japan's intent gave impetus to the drama of their apparently unstoppable push into the Pacific.

Command contortions

I am aiming at three large measures for New Zealand security. First, inducing the United States Navy to give effective protection in the ANZAC area; second, their reinforcement of Fiji and New Caledonia ... and third, the sending of American troops into New Zealand...
— British Prime Minister Sir Winston Churchill, March 1942[60]

New Zealand was not the only South Pacific nation facing a crisis in late 1941. Australia's Northern Territories were directly threatened, and the Labour government of John Curtin wanted to bring remaining Australian forces back from the Middle East.⁶¹ Two of the three divisions were withdrawn,⁶² but in late 1941 the third, 9 Australian Division, was largely pinned down in Tobruk, and it took time to relieve them.⁶³ This came just as British and American authorities tried to sort out mechanisms for administering and fighting the war, including dividing responsibilities at theatre level. Churchill and his staff had rushed to Washington in mid-December 1941 to discuss war strategies. They confirmed the existing agreement to beat Germany first, though Churchill thought it would be 'wrong to speak of our standing on the defensive' in the Pacific and wanted to regain the initiative 'albeit on a minor scale'.⁶⁴

Horse-trading finally put the United States in command of the Pacific, and the main issue was how the two Dominions would fit into this structure.⁶⁵ The question was a legacy of empire; Britain had direct representation on the Joint Chiefs of Staff, but initial plans called for only indirect representation from the Dominions, via a Far Eastern Council in London. This did not go down well in Wellington or Canberra; as Walter Nash noted, 'London is too far from the Pacific to enable a proper appreciation to be made.'⁶⁶ Nor did this guarantee the direct and immediate assistance that both Curtin and Fraser sought. Churchill tried to oil the troubled waters. 'Night and day,' he told Curtin in December 1941, 'I am labouring here to make the best arrangements possible in your interests.'⁶⁷

Curtin wanted action, hinting at independent Australian reliance on US help in a controversial New Year message.⁶⁸ The *New Zealand Herald* applauded the 'forthright terms' with which Curtin outlined his needs, 'burning words' which 'most New Zealanders will readily endorse'.⁶⁹ These sentiments did not echo well in British circles. Churchill feared that the Australian effort to woo favour in Washington might be misinterpreted as a rift with London — this when much of Britain's strength and influence in America derived from the unity of its former empire. 'Do not doubt my loyalty to Australia and New Zealand…' he urged Curtin, 'great ordeals lie before us, but I feel hopeful as never before that we shall emerge safely … from the dark valley.'⁷⁰

The command issue was not resolved until March. After a to-and-fro argument during which Curtin approached Churchill with a proposal to create a united ANZAC Council in Washington, Roosevelt finally suggested that the 'whole of the … responsibility for the Pacific Area will rest on the United States', and that Australia, New Zealand and other local powers would be represented in Washington. He added to Churchill that 'the Pacific Council now sitting in London might well be moved here'.⁷¹ The arrangement left 'all political and governmental matters' in London while 'military matters' were resolved in

Washington. The President promised Churchill a 'close and intimate working relationship' with Australia and New Zealand to ensure their advice was 'in no sense perfunctory but will be considered important and essential'.[72]

As a result the United States accepted what Roosevelt called the 'heavy responsibility ... for the defence of Australia, New Zealand, and sea approaches'.[73] However, this was not a significant concession as US military chiefs had decided that they needed Australia and New Zealand for their own purposes. In December 1941, Marshall had asked the War Plans division to prepare contingency plans in case the Philippines were lost. Brigadier-General Dwight D. Eisenhower, then Deputy Chief of the division, came up with a scheme to springboard operations from Australia. This coincided with MacArthur's thinking and became the basis of American planning. As Roosevelt told Fraser in late March, 'New Zealand and the Fiji islands ... together with Australia, must be held and used as bases for an offensive against Japan.'[74]

Both Dominion governments concurred, and the initiative provided a context within which Churchill was able to persuade the Americans to provide a division each for Australia and New Zealand on top of the forces for the Pacific offensive. He couched these as replacements for the Dominion divisions that were staying in the Middle East, a point clearly directed at Australia. New Zealand already had adequate forces on the ground at home, and Fraser's government had 'never asked for the withdrawal' of 2 NZ Division from the Middle East.[75] Churchill admitted as much to Roosevelt.[76] Nor was the army New Zealand's local priority; as Fraser told Nash, the most effective way to defend the country was to 'intercept any enemy expedition before it reaches New Zealand'.[77] The country needed warships and aircraft, not more men on the ground. From this perspective the more crucial shift was the US decision to springboard their counter-offensives from Australasia — meaning that the United States had to secure both Dominions against invasion. American warships had to be deployed accordingly.

The decision did not guarantee New Zealand a significant role in the counter-offensive, which in early 1942 looked likely to be launched from Australia. New Zealand's involvement actually derived from the inter-service arguments and administrative changes that followed Japan's lightning advances. Wavell's ABDA command was derailed by the Japanese push through the Malay Barrier. A new ANZAC administrative area in the South Pacific was discussed during early 1942 with input from the two Dominions, whose Chiefs of Staff met Lieutenant-General George Brett in Canberra for the purpose. One consequence was the formation of an ANZAC naval squadron under

Australian Admiral G. Crace, broadly comprising the bulk of the RAN and the three major combatants of the RNZN, supported by a US heavy cruiser and two destroyers. The elderly British aircraft carrier *Hermes* was meant to join them, but was sunk in the Indian Ocean by the Japanese before she could reach the South Pacific.[78]

By February the ANZAC area had become problematic in the face of both Japanese advances, and inter-service rivalry in the United States. Australia had become America's front line by default; MacArthur went there in March, and materiel being sent from California was diverted to Brisbane. This was in line with Eisenhower's ideas, but did not resolve the main argument. MacArthur wanted an army campaign, pushing through New Guinea and back into the Philippines. Nimitz preferred a naval strategy. A compromise split the Pacific into two commands: a South-West Pacific area under MacArthur, based on Australia; and a South Pacific area under Rear-Admiral Robert Ghormley, which included New Zealand and the islands north and west to the Solomons. This put New Zealand under US Navy authority, which initially did not find favour in Wellington. Fraser viewed Australia and New Zealand as a single strategic entity and protested to Admiral E.J. King, US Chief of Naval Operations, adding that the proposals also threw control of the New Zealand brigade in Fiji into question — he wanted the United States to consult the New Zealand government before they were moved.[79]

However, the split did have a positive spin-off. New Zealand was the only developed nation in the South Pacific administrative area, and became the main base for US operations into the Solomons. This guaranteed that New Zealand would become home not only to the division intended for direct defence, but also the larger forces intended for operations in the islands, along with the extensive command, control and logistics apparatus that went with them.

The benefit of even transitory US forces for local defence was obvious — as was the implied extension of US naval forces to protect them — and the government considered New Zealand was vulnerable until they arrived. By March an uneasy Fraser believed Japanese forces were 'free for further adventures', though again his focus remained on air and sea defence — he asked for naval forces and fighter aircraft as well as more men.[80] Nash, now in Washington, spent an hour with US Army Chief of Staff General George C. Marshall and discovered that a division was due to leave the United States on 20 May for New Zealand — but there was no immediate answer on the aircraft.[81] US staff planners concurred that New Zealand's defence was 'primarily a naval problem' and were of the opinion that assault on New

Zealand was virtually impossible while the United States Navy's Pacific Fleet remained intact. However, if Japan did act, the Americans now feared that an assault could include six or seven divisions and a 'very large naval force'.[82] This scale was dramatically higher than suggested in prior assessments, and from the perspective of policy-makers in Wellington everything consequently swung on the US Pacific Fleet remaining undefeated.

These command changes did not prevent the ANZAC squadron from forming at Suva in mid-February. Tasks included convoy escort, either as a squadron or by individual detachments, and operations in support of Task Force 11, which included the large US aircraft carrier USS *Lexington*. The New Zealand contribution was significant; during February, for instance, *Leander* steamed 7546 miles during 24 continuous days at sea, *Achilles* notched up 6703 miles and 21 days; and *Monowai* steamed 7588 miles in 20 days away from port.[83]

These were not the only RNZN activities during these crucial months. The minesweeper *Gale* deployed to Fiji in December 1941, replacing the *Viti* and beginning nearly five years' continuous service by RNZN minesweepers in the islands. They ranged from Fiji to the Solomons and were employed in tasks from convoy escort to beach patrol and anti-submarine work. Ships involved in this ongoing campaign included purpose-built 'Castle' class sweepers as well as converted trawlers and vessels such as the former Wellington harbour ferry *Muritai*.[84] Other minesweeping and anti-submarine work was simultaneously carried out in New Zealand local waters.

The turn of the tide

By early 1942 Japan was established from Manchuria to Burma, Java and the Solomons. Where next was a moot point. Army command wanted to secure the southern perimeter by taking Port Moresby and the island chains to the east, but the Naval General Staff preferred a thrust into India and Ceylon, or a direct assault on Australia. Yamamoto thought priority should be given to eliminating the US Pacific Fleet, restricting US activities to their west coast until at least late 1943. The result was a compromise plan to take New Guinea and Tulagi in May, followed by an assault on Midway and the Aleutians in June — which Yamamoto hoped would draw the remaining ships of the US Pacific fleet into a decisive battle in which he would destroy it. This would be followed by a surge into New Caledonia, Fiji and Samoa, isolating Australasia and creating what was called a 'ribbon defence'. The United States would have no option but to attack there, or risk being flanked if they instead pushed directly across the central Pacific.

Major-General Tomitaro Horii was appointed to command the South Seas Detachment Force for the attack on Port Moresby. The island was geographically complex, its central highlands a morass of rugged mountains that posed a difficult barrier to an advancing army. The only alternative was by sea, and a powerful naval force was organised to escort the invasion convoy in early May.

US cryptanalysts had partly broken Japan's JN-25 naval code and were aware of these moves; the only unknown was the target of the northern thrust, but through a subterfuge, the Americans discovered it was Midway. US Pacific Fleet Commander in Chief Admiral Chester W. Nimitz deployed his forces accordingly, sending the aircraft carriers *Lexington* and *Yorktown* to the South Pacific under command of Rear-Admiral Frank Fletcher. A massive battle followed in the Coral Sea, fought over four days from 4 May. It was the first engagement in history between opposing carrier forces, and the ANZAC squadron was heavily involved, though without its New Zealand component — the cruisers had been detached for essential convoy work. Tactically it was a draw; Japan lost the small carrier *Shoho* and 105 aircraft, a lighter blow than the loss to America of the 44,000 ton *Lexington* and 81 aircraft. However, the Port Moresby invasion force turned back; and to that extent the Allies fulfilled their strategic objectives.[85]

The focus switched to the central Pacific, where Yamamoto hoped to capture Midway Island as the bait with which to trigger a decisive showdown. The force he deployed for the purpose was vastly more powerful than the US Pacific Fleet. However, the Americans had several aces up their sleeve. Yamamoto did not know that the United States had broken his codes and that the Pacific Fleet would intervene before the invasion began. Nor did he think that Fletcher had three carriers — *Yorktown* was supposed to be at the bottom of the Coral Sea. As a result the opposing air strengths were similar: around 350 American carrier and land-based aircraft against 325 Japanese.[86]

Even so, the outcome was largely a matter of fate. Against the odds, a dozen US dive-bombers managed to hit the fleet carriers of Vice-Admiral Nagumo Chuichi's Carrier Striking Force, which were littered with fuel lines and bombs as they prepared for a strike after several hours' vacillation. The results were decisive. In just five minutes three of the carriers were reduced to burning wrecks; and a further strike later in the day dealt with the fourth and last.

Yamamoto still had vast surface superiority, but the loss of the entire Carrier Striking Force was a heavy blow, and in the early hours of 5 June he decided to abandon the attack.[87]

Midway was the turning point of the Pacific war. Yamamoto's Combined Fleet still ruled the waves for the moment, but Japan had lost the initiative. They never regained it. In point of fact, the clock had been ticking in an industrial sense as early as 1940 when the US authorised its initial major naval build-up. United States warship construction planned for 1942 alone totalled 2.6 million tons. Japan managed less than a tenth of that. The following year US warship construction outstripped that of Japan 14-fold. Other American production in 1943 included 12.5 million tons of merchant shipping, 85,900 aircraft and 29,500 tanks.[88] This was achieved through a variety of measures that included US government control of national labour resources from the start of the 1942 fiscal year, rationing, and — the following year — state control of wages and prices.

CHAPTER THREE

Into the Islands

> ...the best course ... in furthering the security of New Zealand is to participate to the fullest extent in offensive operations against the Japanese, and at the same time leave nothing undone to strengthen the forces for home defence.
> — Lieutenant-General Sir Edward Puttick, 3 August 1942.[1]

Defeat at Midway threw Japan's military temporarily into disarray. From the army perspective the thrust to Samoa could not take place, and defence of existing conquests was considered almost impossible. However, the navy still hoped to force the Americans to a negotiated peace, wanted to secure the Solomons to protect the main naval base at Truk,[2] and was able to get their way. One consequence was a second army effort to take Port Moresby, this time overland. Work also turned to building defensive positions in the Solomons, including a seaplane base at Tulagi.[3] In July, Japanese forces landed on Guadalcanal and began constructing an airstrip there.

There were other divisions of opinion on the Allied side. MacArthur was determined to oppose the Japanese in New Guinea and roll them back to the Philippines. Nimitz preferred a central Pacific campaign, leaving Japan's South Pacific forces to wither in isolation. Both schemes had to be reconciled with the need to stop the Japanese in the Solomons, a strategy that could then be extended into a counter-offensive.

These political machinations did not slow the start of the Solomons strategy, which had been under development since May and was urgently needed to secure the supply routes to Australia. Operation Watchtower — nicknamed 'Shoestring' by the men — was scheduled for August 1942 even before the Midway victory.[4] The US intended to use New Zealand as the base of the effort, which is primarily why forces were sent there. And as far as Fraser was concerned, New Zealand had to join in. The issue was:

> ...not only a question of the immediate security of our own shores and our island territories; we must also take the long view and ensure that when the future of the Pacific is being considered after the war we ... are in the most favourable possible political position.[5]

Actually participating was another matter. The RNZN had been fully involved in the Pacific war since December, and this work continued without pause. However, plans to develop the RNZAF for a combat role — 'primarily for supporting amphibious and naval operations' but, again, to show New Zealand willingness 'to assist in every way'[6] — were hampered by lack of equipment. Britain could offer nothing. Fraser hoped Ghormley might 'assume full responsibility for ... the development and equipment of all our forces'[7] when he arrived in May 1942. King, however, had ordered Ghormley not to do so. This came as a surprise in New Zealand and Fraser thought King might have misunderstood earlier stipulations about control of New Zealand forces. Part of the problem was certainly 'enciphering errors' in the to-and-fro correspondence with Nash in Washington,[8] but it appeared there had also been a misunderstanding in New Zealand. The New Zealand Chiefs of Staff believed they would be reporting to Ghormley 'for the land defence of New Zealand' — meaning that New Zealand was also on the US supply chain — and were not disabused of the notion until Ghormley told them at their first meeting.[9]

The implication affected everything from equipment to air defence, and while some of these issues could 'no doubt be settled locally',[10] the implications for the RNZAF seemed dire. Fraser asked Nash to clarify the point, if necessary directly with King, adding:

> ...you should make clear to him [King] that it was never our desire to exclude any of our forces from the South Pacific Command, and that we are anxious that these forces shall play a part in future offensive operations as far as they may be required to do so ... and that they should be trained and equipped in co-ordination with United States forces with this object in view.[11]

Fraser wanted a 'forward plan' to expand the RNZAF to 'say, twenty modern squadrons of the required types by 1943', and he wanted the United States to 'accept responsibility for the equipment and development'. He also thought that the RNZAF itself should be 'principally aligned to naval operations' and 'consequently under naval command'.[12]

The issue was batted around between New Zealand, US and British Chiefs of Staff for several months; but the outcome was inevitably at the mercy of American planners, who settled in August for a ten-squadron combat force based principally around P-40 Kittyhawk fighters and Hudson patrol bombers. King was reluctant to increase the allocation, stipulating that additional aircraft would have to come from British production. Ghormley was given control of the forces in September.[13]

This set the basis for a sustained New Zealand air and sea contribution to the Pacific conflict, which was maintained to the end of the war. The RNZAF eventually expanded beyond its 1942 limitations and had particular priority for available resources — in June the War Cabinet gave air force and navy first and second place respectively in the queue for manpower, including contributions to equivalent British services. Organising a land force was another matter. The army was at the bottom of the chain, below war production, and this brought other issues into the calculation. Manpower was a problem by 1942, and government wanted to focus the army effort in Europe. This was not for sentimental reasons. New Zealand relied absolutely on Britain for practical prosperity in the 1940s, and Savage's early catch phrase 'where Britain goes, we go' was an effective summary of the financial and economic realities. A future dominated by a Nazi-controlled Europe was going to be bleak, and there was no option but to fight there — mainly on land with 2 NZ Division, but also by manpower contribution to the RAF via the pilot training scheme, the Fleet Air Arm, Royal Navy and the Royal Marines. While the practical scale of contribution in a strategic sense was not large, the political effect was potentially significant for New Zealand.

The problem was that there was insufficient resource to do both that and fight a tri-service war in the Pacific. On the other hand, the war cabinet felt compelled — and also, in part, for political reasons — to contribute to the Pacific war in every respect. The result was a decision to organise a land force for that theatre on top of the air and sea contributions, at least until the need to reinforce 2 NZ Division or other developments prevented it. Size and role of the force were less clear. King suggested after the Midway victory that New Zealand's Fiji-based brigade might train with an American amphibious division 'with a view to eventual participation in offensive operations'.[14] What this meant was unclear; King hinted at garrison duties. Puttick thought they might join MacArthur's New Guinea campaign.[15]

Either way, it met the political aims Fraser had in mind, and the War Cabinet gave Puttick authority to begin discussions on 24 July. He met Ghormley at the end of the month to go through the possibilities. The American commander preferred four 'alternative forces' — only one of which was divisional-sized — to 'meet any contingency at short notice'.[16] Puttick plumped for the largest — a three-brigade sized 'D' — as 'our target for planning' and recommended using New Zealand's 7600-odd strong Fiji brigade 'as the basis' with additional input 'from existing New Zealand formations'.[17] The Allied position had 'improved', and he could not 'conceive any probability of an invasion of New Zealand at this stage'.[18]

Time was short if the men were to join the Guadalcanal campaign, and Puttick suggested that the 'scope and nature of the operations justifies the acceptance of ... incompletely trained troops'.[19] In the event this proved over-ambitious, and Ghormley finally asked for a smaller two-brigade force, Kiwi 'C', which he wanted in New Caledonia as soon as possible, preparatory to garrison duties further into the islands and possible front-line work alongside US forces.

Wellington to Guadalcanal

While these discussions went on, US forces prepared to attack Guadalcanal. New Zealand was the only industrialised country in the South Pacific administrative area and became the prime base for the assault; King even asked whether landing craft could be assembled there.[20] On 13 June the USS *Wakefield* brought the lead elements of 1 Marine Division, under Major-General Alexander Vandergrift, to the capital. They arrived just one day after elements of 37 Division reached Auckland — the separate force promised to defend New Zealand. Preparing for the marine assault was a race against time,[21] particularly as all the cargo intended to nourish the campaign had to be hauled out of the freighters, landed on Aotea Quay, then reloaded in the right order. A dockside strike did not help.

The marines were based at Paraparaumu, where the Public Works Department spent six weeks building barracks. Although victory at Midway eased the risks of operations into the Pacific, Ghormley brought the attack forward as soon as he heard of the new airfield on Guadalcanal. He had nearly 20,000 marines under Vandergrift, and naval forces that included three carriers, the new battleship *North Carolina*, six cruisers and supporting destroyers. The assault force accumulated in Wellington harbour and sailed for Fiji on 22 July, screened by cruisers and destroyers — including the three cruisers of the Royal Australian Navy.[22]

Ghormley's schedule gave no time to train properly, nor had the disparate naval forces worked closely together before. Rehearsals off Fiji at the end of July revealed problems, and the landing was deferred from 4 to 7 August. The marines finally stormed ashore on Guadalcanal without opposition, but the same was not true across the channel at Tulagi, where marines attacked next day in the face of heavy resistance. Vice-Admiral Mikawa Gunichi counter-attacked the invasion fleet on the night of 7 August, savaging the Allied escorts.[23] This tipped the local naval balance in Japan's favour, and Rear-Admiral Richmond K. Turner decided to withdraw the transports to Noumea before they had unloaded much heavy equipment, leaving Vandergrift's forces with little chance of immediate succour. In mid-August the Japanese began pouring reinforcements into Guadalcanal, mostly from 35 Infantry Brigade under Major-General Kawaguchi Kiyotake.[24]

Yamamoto moved part of the Combined Fleet south to support them, and a series of costly naval battles followed during September and October.[25] The RNZN was directly involved; the cruiser *Leander* sailed for Espiritu Santo and joined Task Force 64, under command of Rear-Admiral C.H. Wright, almost immediately escorting a convoy with 5000 troops to Guadalcanal. The force reached the island on 18 September, covered the transports as they unloaded, and departed just after nightfall — missing a Japanese squadron by some hours.[26]

As the battle for the island drew in more and more Japanese resources, the decision was taken at Imperial General Headquarters to suspend operations in New Guinea and focus instead on the Solomons. These preparations peaked in mid-November, when the Japanese tried to land 28 Division, supporting the landings with a powerful task force that included two older but modernised battlecruisers, now re-classified as fast battleships. They clashed with a US task force over several nights in mid-November — and were decisively defeated.[27] The initiative passed to the United States, but this did not prevent Japan continuing to run men and equipment into Guadalcanal at night by destroyer — operations nicknamed 'rat runs' or, more benignly, the 'Tokyo Express'. Other stores were shifted by submarine; and although outnumbered, Japanese forces ashore often fought to the death.

It was the end of the year before Japanese command decided to abandon Guadalcanal to the Americans — and February 1943 before the island was evacuated.[28] Even then it was far from secure, and isolated soldiers harassed Allied forces there for months.

3 NZ Division is deployed

Plans to deploy Kiwi 'C' into the Pacific were pushed ahead during mid-1942, though by September even Kiwi 'A' was six weeks off being trained to basic combat standards.[29] Other troops were needed to garrison Norfolk Island and Tonga, and Puttick finally had to recommend that only a portion of Kiwi 'C' could go,[30] about 80 percent of the intended establishment.[31] The rest would follow, including 'an armoured regiment', which Puttick wanted 'despatched at first opportunity'.[32] Six weeks worth of exercises in the Waikato concluded in mid-October with the so-called 'Battle of the Kaimais', a realistic mock campaign through some of New Zealand's toughest terrain. It rained for 'the greater part' of the six-day exercise,[33] but the men did well — although Barrowclough thought some behaved as if they were the 'Tararua tramping club making a road'.[34]

The force — still officially Kiwi 'C' — assembled in New Caledonia over three months from November 1942. Barrowclough did not like the composition. Garrison duties had 'probably long since ceased to be important', but they still had heavy coast defence and anti-aircraft artillery, 'which is normally not part of a British division'.[35] There seemed every possibility that the force might be asked to relieve one of the three US divisions on Guadalcanal, and Barrowclough wanted a three-brigade division for the purpose.[36] This was not the only consideration. New Zealand General Staff passed Barrowclough's request on to the War Cabinet with the comment that although the plan would add 'approximately 3000 men to the manpower calculations', the 'extra fire-power and more balanced organisation … might possibly result in less casualties, and in the long run a saving in the calls on manpower.' The Deputy Chief of General Staff, Major-General Sir Keith Stewart, added that, 'Apart from manpower considerations, the experiences of this war, including that of the 2nd Division at Sidi Rezegh in 1941, have proved that a two-brigade division and two-battalion brigades are militarily unsound.'[37]

In early February 1943 the War Cabinet endorsed a proposal to bring 3 NZ Division up to full strength. Troops were scoured from other establishments, some garrisons — such as the Norfolk Island force — replaced with Grade II men, and men as young as 20 were allowed to serve on garrison duty providing they had written parental consent. Men over 41 were allowed to volunteer for similar service. All these moves freed combat-grade men for the division. However, talk of raising a Maori battalion for Pacific service was tempered by fears of American discrimination — US forces were fully segregated,[38] and there had been problems in New Zealand. As one soldier recalled, the 'Yanks idea of racism ... caused a lot of bad feeling between the heroes of Guadalcanal and the Maori Battalion so that there were street brawls between Yanks and our native soldiers...'[39]

Final arrangements were hammered out by Gordon Coates, who met Halsey in Noumea on 24 February. The US commander wanted the New Zealanders to 'proceed ... at once' with their plans, including the Maori battalion — he 'and all his staff' discounted 'entirely' the possibility that US forces might discriminate against Maori.[40] The bureaucratic wheels were in motion by early March and 2 Maori Battalion was formally approved in April. However, the Maori War Effort Parliamentary Committee thought new recruits should be 'directly supporting their kinsmen' in the Middle East; while the US Military Attaché in Wellington, Colonel J.H. Nankivell, felt it was 'unwise' to have Maori serve alongside US forces despite Halsey's assurances.[41] In the end the Maori were sent to Egypt, though the driving factor behind that decision was the need to replace Maori brought home by the furlough scheme rather than concerns about US attitudes.[42]

This scheme also torpedoed any chance of a three-brigade division in the Pacific. In theory it was designed to give the veterans of 2NZEF a holiday; but replacements had to be provided and Puttick warned Barrowclough as early as May 1943 that it 'may cause your reinforcements to be taken'.[43] Although Puttick was of the opinion that both divisions should be maintained 'to the last gasp' even if that meant reducing war establishments,[44] government policy formally prioritised the air contribution, then naval operations, both including contributions to British service. Production followed — and the army came last.[45] This was not the only difficulty. The first furlough draft showed little inclination to return to Europe; there were mutinies among those slated to go back. Replacements had to be found.[46]

Barrowclough was still determined to get the men he needed. The decision to bring 3 NZ Division up to strength 'has had a very marked effect on the morale of this force,' he reported. 'The belief that we shall eventually be given an active role ... has resulted in an unbelievable improvement in our state of training and readiness for war.' He wondered whether 2 NZ Division might not be reduced for garrison duties instead.[47] Tactical demands finally forced a decision. 'Have reason to believe we may be asked to undertake an active mission involving the whole Divison about the end of July,' Barrowclough reported near the end of May. 'Think it would be disastrous if we were not in a position to accept.'[48] Two days later Harmon's representative, Colonel W. Bassett, confirmed that the Kiwis would be needed at the 'end of July', although Barrowclough thought 'actual events' would be delayed by 'two or three weeks'.[49]

Getting 3 NZ Division up to strength became urgent. Puttick suggested adding a Fijian battalion, and put the idea to Halsey with the rider that 'the manpower situation here ... makes it impossible for New Zealand to maintain two divisions and an expanded air force overseas ... I consider the Fijians very valuable for jungle warfare...'[50] Halsey declined; if forces were moved from Fiji they would have to be replaced with American troops.[51] Puttick argued the point, finally pointing out that there was 'no prospect of completing the division from our own resources', and that if Fijian troops could not be used it would reduce 3 NZ Division to a 'two-brigade division'.[52] Halsey — 'with great reluctance'[53] — decided that would have to happen, a decision Barrowclough also 'regretted'. But he felt it was 'essential [that] we should accept the two-brigade basis rather than refuse the proposals for active employment'.[54]

The War Cabinet approved the move on 27 June, fixing 3 NZ Division at two brigades with a total establishment of 15,837 men,[55] plus 2000-odd reinforcements for an ultimate — and final — total of 17,831.[56] There were no more. As Fraser remarked, New Zealand could not 'reinforce Barrowclough beyond the number he already has in his pool'.[57] The decision meant disbanding a battalion each of the Ruahine and Scots Regiments, which Barrowclough accepted 'only because it was inevitable'.[58] The point was driven home to the US commander by Colonel C.W. Salmon of the New Zealand Chiefs of Staff.[59] Halsey protested, telling Fraser he was:

> *greatly disappointed that New Zealand could not furnish a division with three full brigades, and accepted the decision on two brigades with great reluctance ... I am counting on you to furnish such additional replacements as may be necessary to maintain these two brigades at full strength.*[60]

Fraser told him it was impossible. The country had been fighting for four years. 'Grade A' men were 'practically exhausted' and it was impossible to do more than 'we are now doing'. Furthermore, unless there was a change of policy, the two brigades of 3 NZ Division would also be disbanded 'when the

reinforcement pool in New Zealand has been exhausted', in order to maintain 2 NZ Division in Europe.⁶¹ Halsey had to accept.

While these debates went on the division settled into New Caledonia. It was home not just to the combat forces of the divison but also the base personnel of the Second New Zealand Expeditionary Force in the Pacific (2 NZEFIP): the administrators, doctors, nurses, engineers, clerks and others essential to running the military machine. Divisional headquarters were set up at Bourail, north of Noumea, and the No. 4 General Hospital was initially established nearby in the Bougen River valley. 'We lost a lot of sweat here, road-making,' one soldier wrote home.⁶² Other facilities and depots were built in the vicinity. Even soldiers' clubs were set up, following the practice adopted in Egypt. The Kiwi Club on Bourail Beach and the Bourail Club were effectively hotels with overnight accommodation. Some 2,580 men of all ranks finally worked at the base.

The island came under command of US Major-General Am Patch, who asked the New Zealanders to defend the northern area. Barrowclough spread the division accordingly; 14 Brigade went to Taom in the north, divisional headquarters near Poya, 15 Brigade — before it was disbanded — at Bourail; and 8 Brigade at Bouloupari.

New Caledonia had attractions for men who had expected to face the winter from poorly insulated army huts near Te Awamutu; but there were also hazards. Dengue fever, parasites, infection, dysentery, sunburn and dehydration all posed risks, and men were urged not to put their heads under water for fear of collecting parasites or being cut by floating coral particles. The small injuries were easily infected, and in 1943 the best treatment remained sulpha drugs, which were marginally effective and carried side-effects.[63]

Mosquitoes made life miserable. 'Spanner is catching a mozzie to squash on his letter and send home,' Ted Skinner wrote home one afternoon. '[I] Just squashed one on my ear, he came down with a roar like a dive-bomber. There is a steady drone in the tent now & I must retreat under the net. Here we go again.' Later he interrupted his note. 'Must knock off a moment & swat a lone raider in the net.'[64] The constant battle was interrupted only by inclement weather. 'Here comes the first mozzie bomber since the rain started yesterday,' he wrote later to his wife in early October. 'There will be more in a minute. The moonlight nights you talk of are best spent in our nets. Don't be alarmed if when I come home I start slapping myself from force of habit.'[65] He was not alone. 'We are still pestered with the mosquitoes & they are worse than ever down here,' Harry Waterman wrote. 'I suppose we will get away from them some day.'[66]

Water was heavily chlorinated, a precaution which — as Skinner pointed out — made the tea 'practically undrinkable', and which he thought was 'unnecessary as the boiling purifies it'. The tropical rain beat down on the roof as he wrote, reminding him of the rivers back home in Hawke's Bay.[67]

Food was another matter. Army rations were hardly *haute cuisine*, and the men improvised. 'We have been busy cleaning up some ration dumps,' Ted Skinner wrote. 'Casting a lot of tinned fruit & milk away to burn because it has gone bad, but there is quite a lot in amongst it which is sound so we have been eating fruit cocktail & Australian cling peaches until we are sick of them.'[68] Wild deer had been plentiful before the war and were still easy to find in 1943. Some even wandered through the camp.[69] Venison made a pleasant change from 'stringy old corned beef'.[70] They were not the only wildlife preyed on by hungry New Zealanders. 'There are some wild pigs here in the bush beside our camp,' Waterman reported to his family one day in May 'they have two in the sty & we killed one today so we will have pork for tea tomorrow night…'[71] Local restaurants offered other variations. Waterman went with one group across the island to a hotel:

> which was run by French people & it was a very nice tea too. We had soup & steak, beans, macaroni & bread & then came the fruit. It was mandarins & it was very nice. The meal cost us 85 cents & a bottle of wine was put on the table for eight of us which cost five dollars between us, so it was a good day out & the best I've had on the island.[72]

The French influence was clear in Noumea, a town of 11,000 souls where settlers and troops far outnumbered locals during the day. The cultural and ethnic mix included a significant percentage of Indo-Chinese brought over under French administration. This exotic, polyglot, tropical edition of Europe was a far cry from the streets of Auckland or Wellington. US and New Zealand soldiers found it 'pleasant to sit in the town square' watching 'bare-footed Javanese women in their multi-coloured sarongs'.[73] French-speaking New Zealanders suddenly became valuable. Ted Skinner had volunteered for the army in the hope of eventually getting to England, but his fluent French prompted army administrators to put him with 3 NZ Division.

Many New Zealand units were stationed cheek-by-jowl alongside US forces, and American cooks introduced the New Zealanders to 'the doughboys diet — flapjacks and maple syrup' with 'cawfee' in place of tea. The Kiwis soon picked up baseball; but the cultural exchange cut both ways — the Americans adopted cricket.[74] Meanwhile the men of 1 Scots built an open-air theatre, in which the 37 Battalion concert party put up a 'really good' performance of their 'Houailou follies' in late March. The audience was impressed, 'not a single dud item in it and some really beautiful singers'. A motorcycle on the hill behind provided stage lighting.[75] The show included a ballet performance, complete with costumes, made up of some of the 'toughest eggs in the battalion'.[76]

Tough eggs were needed for what followed. Route marches in the heat left the men staggering. Two sections of Ted Skinner's unit, the 1st Scots, were sent 'away around the hills' one day in mid-March, trudging along in blazing heat until they came to a waterfall, 'the first time I have had a reasonably cold drink on the island,' he wrote afterwards. 'On the way home we called at a natives place to buy some fruit but there was no-one at home. There are plenty of wild orange trees here and they will be ripe in about a fortnight.'[77] A week later he was on fatigues. 'The rest have gone out on manoeuvres today ... the others think I am lucky as they have about a 70lb pack to carry.'[78]

The army joined a detachment of RNZAF 4 Squadron, operating from an airfield on the Plaine des Gaiacs. They had arrived at the request of Rear Admiral John R. McCain, commanding US air forces in the South Pacific (COMAIRSOPAC), who asked the RNZAF to supplement anti-submarine patrols around New Caledonia. Two Vincents were despatched from Fiji, while ground crews under Squadron Leader C.J. Kidson left New Zealand in July 1942 on board the *Mackinac*, arrived off Noumea on 5 July and were trucked 180 miles (300 km) to the airfield. Equipment was short. Prefabricated huts, vehicles and emergency rations were supplied from stocks in New Zealand — the squadron had to have 21 days worth to hand, though ordinary supplies were expected to come from US forces. By November 1942 the RNZAF force on the island comprised 281 of all ranks, with 12 Hudsons; and it remained in New Caledonia until March 1943.[79]

Naval and air action in the Solomons

Air Force and Navy carried New Zealand's front-line action during the early part of the Solomons campaign. As the Guadalcanal campaign gained momentum during September 1942, US Colonel F.G. Schneider of the Commanding General South Pacific office (COMGENSOPAC) told RNZAF air staff that 'General Harmon was anxious to have an additional squadron ... located at the Plains des Gaiacs [sic] ...'[80] It happened that No. 3 Squadron was available, but US authorities changed the destination first to Vila, and then Espiritu Santo. This was less straightforward, and Group Captain Arthur de T. Nevill, Deputy Chief of Air Staff, flew to the island and saw Harmon personally. He was told that the squadron was required for reconnaissance work. There was no time to send an advance party to reconnoitre, but Nevill looked for himself and reported that a wide range of gear was needed, including mosquito netting, water tanks, beds and timber.

Deployment was conducted at relatively short notice with the inter-island ferries and a merchant, under what Nevill called 'very difficult circumstances, chiefly owing to the ignorance and vacillation of our friends'. He thought the 'branches did remarkably well under such conditions'.[81] A draft history took a different view. 'A fair criticism would be that a lack of anticipation had been shown in planning at a high level.'[82] *Wahine* left Auckland on 22 September and reached Vela, the largest town on the island of Efate in the New Hebrides, four days later.

Here they saw their first signs of war. John Morgan, one of the ground engineers, wrote that they were:

> *Alongside [the] tanker early. Not many houses in sight. Very mountainous looking show, with plenty of bush and palms, also several locals rowing around in outrigger canoes. Pulled in alongside tanker & spent most of day refuelling. Pulled away and anchored until 1745. Several boys started fishing over side, but though many fish were about, caught none. Lot of mixing with Yanks on tanker going on… A lot of Yank planes around. A dozen in formation in morning, a couple of Fortresses & 3 or 4 float-planes…* [83]

Taybank left New Zealand on 25 September with 317 tons of equipment, and the squadron set up camp at the muddy north end of Pallukula airfield on Espiritu Santo. The place had a 'bad reputation which lasted until the end of the war'.[84] Nothing was organised. Medical stores did not come ashore for days. 'When they did,' Warrant Officer M. Harris recalled on interview after the war 'it was found that none of the stuff ordered had been sent'.[85] The aircraft — 13 Hudsons — arrived soon afterwards under Wing Commander G.H. Fisher. US authorities expected the squadron to take over anti-submarine patrols in the Segond Channel, the main Allied anchorage; but even this was not straightforward. British-specification bomb racks had to be modified to carry American depth charges. Morgan spent most of 13 October 'fitting carriers & putting on special ones for VS 325 lb depth bombs (had to cut nicks out of main spar!!) Heat pretty terrific. Dirty as all hell too.'[86]

Espiritu Santo became the RNZAF's main Pacific base for the duration, home to the No. 1 (Islands) Group Headquarters, initially under Group Captain Sidney Wallingford. Life settled into routine marked with intermittent action and inclement weather. The tropical rains were the worst. 'Place like a bog,' Morgan penned after heavy rain in late October. 'Sat around most of day, but filled in part of time making up belts. Strict blackout at night. Clearly heard what was probably sea battle going on. … F. O'Neill on guard said he saw many gun flashes in sky.'[87] Others were less relaxed:

> *My nerves are all to blazes these days — the runway is hell — very narrow between the palms & we have nearly had several crashes & one can only stand a certain amount. … However I'm racehorse fit — the food is quite good & our Air Crew*

chaps are the best lads I've ever known so I've much to be thankful for. But I would like a decent bath![88]

A wider combat role had to wait on Curtis P-40 fighters being supplied under lend-lease. The RNZAF was not a high priority. However, in October, Harmon suggested that New Zealand crews could use the P-40s abandoned in Tongatapu by a departing US Army Air Force pursuit squadron. The Tonga group were on the main convoy route from the United States to Australia and New Zealand.[89] Wing Commander E.M. Lewis flew to Fumota airfield and discovered that the New Zealanders would have to supply everything except the aircraft, but it was an opportunity not to be missed, and No. 15 Squadron formed at a cracking pace under Squadron Leader A. Crichton. 'They pumped me (and some others) full of injections,' one of the men recalled 'and gave me leave from 4.30 pm on that same day until 7.00 pm that night to say my good byes.'[90]

The squadron departed Wellington on the *President Jackson* and reached Tongatapu after dark on 27 October. The grass strip at Fumota had been built by the New Zealand Public Works Department, and 'was not easy to detect until extension runways of coral had been laid'.[91] The bad news was that the 23 aircraft were 'worn out crates…'[92] Everything needed repairing. 'The first thing our men noticed was that not one machine gun on the planes was serviceable owing to rust and coral dust etc,' Basil Berry wrote.[93] There were only 15 spare engines on the island and no parts apart from spark plugs, but in a round-the-clock effort the engineers got the aircraft flyable. Patrols began a few days later – and the squadron immediately had its first tragedy. 'One of the young pilots was flying too low and the plane crashed into bush upside down and caught fire.'[94]

15 Squadron operated from Tongatapu until early 1943. Racks were eventually provided for the 325-lb depth bombs. For the most part the dawn-and-dusk square searches proved fruitless, although:

> *on one occasion a Jap ship was thought to be in the vicinity which caused a good flap, especially for the armourers and Flight Sergeant Hawkins, as they had to bomb up six Kittys with 500 lb AP and no-one knew anything about fusing [the] Americans bombs.*[95]

The island had many attractions for off-duty airmen. To be able to pick and eat fresh fruit was a new experience for many and something, Berry recalled, that they could have done with later on Guadalcanal. The Tongans were 'very friendly ... and would give us native mats of Tapa cloth and shell beads ... but after the Americans would pay them any price they asked they soon found out the value of the almighty dollar and there were no more free gifts'.[96] Mail was a problem. 'Letter mail was fairly frequent,' Berry wrote 'but parcels and newspapers failed to arrive'. It turned out that the mail was going to Espiritu Santo, where the accumulated pile was eventually burnt. The squadron moved there in February 1943, deploying with special belly-tanks and 'Dumbo' floatplane escort. The first over-ocean hop of 195 minutes took them to Nadi; then they flew four hours to Efate before a final hour-long flight to Espiritu Santo. This was not without its risks: the Nadi-Efate leg was a substantial over-water distance and apparently the longest over-sea ferry mission by single-engined fighter aircraft to that time.

The RNZAF deployed further afield in November 1942, when six No. 3 Squadron Hudsons and two spare aircrews were sent to Guadalcanal, joining more than 100 US aircraft on Henderson Field and coming under operational control of Brigadier-General L.E. Woods. The squadron was attached to the Search and Patrol Group of Task Force 63's Air Search and Attack Command, charged with finding Japanese ships running supplies into the island. On the first day, Flying Officer G.E. Gudsell and crew located a small convoy escorted by a destroyer near Vella Lavella. Three days later Gudsell's Hudson was ambushed by three fighters while he tried to investigate another Japanese force near that island. Gudsell rallied his crew and the aircraft survived the 17-minute engagement that followed. On 2 December, west of New Georgia, Flight Sergeant I.M. Page dropped his Hudson low to investigate what he thought was a canoe. It was actually a small submarine, and Page pressed an attack, dropping two 250-pound bombs and two depth charges. The Japanese boat crash-dived, but although one bomb fell on the vessel as it went under and a patch of oil was observed on the surface, the 'kill' could not be confirmed. An RNZAF Hudson also launched the first attack on a new Japanese airfield at Munda, on New Georgia island just 150 miles from Guadalcanal.

Richard Andrew arrived on Guadalcanal in late December, finding the place 'definitely much hotter' than Espiritu Santo:

> Last night for instance ... I spent an hour digging a drain round our tent & after that I just sweated for an hour ... The drinking water of course has been cleaned but it's cool & very drinkable. This is such an important thing for one keeps his bottle with him and is at it all the time. I must tell you while speaking of meals that

we get the most marvellous coffee — it's half canned milk & half coffee & it's really beautiful. I get generally two enormous cups full & I feel I could live on it.[97]

Christmas came, and with it 500 cigarettes per man from the Americans. John Morgan 'thought it decent of them to include us'. Christmas Day on the island was a liquid affair:

Told after photo parade that we would be getting 2 quart bottles of hooch issued free at 4 pm. Cut 2 out before tea, one of my own & one got by impersonating non-drinker, Vic Connell. Fred O'Neill, Laurie Easton did same by posing as two more non-drinkers. Got pretty boisterous affair at night. Good feed dished up by Sgts. Bit of singing going on in mess. CO made a speech, but is as unpopular as hell & got cold shoulder. Got back and found Yank met today back in tent with books … Went to his tent for a visit & spent a couple of hours. Took his tentmates down at "Blackjack" … Yank name for Pontoon. Good bloke, name of Bob More, from Kentucky. Pumped couple of beers into him. Got back & made own supper. Then Newton went to Yank camp with me. Supper in our tent pretty boisterous with lot of ballet dancing & other foolery.[98]

Ongoing naval operations took centre stage that month. Both the RNZN's cruisers had been hard-worked through the year, and although *Leander* was scheduled to spend time in the islands, she had to return to Auckland instead for urgent repairs.[99] *Achilles* was scheduled for a modernisation refit in Britain in 1943, but was meanwhile available for Pacific service and sent to Espiritu Santo in mid-December, where she joined Task Force 67. The small anti-submarine minesweepers *Kiwi*, *Moa*, *Tui* and *Matai* also reached the Solomons at the end of 1942 and were soon on patrol near the landing area. J.L.W. Salter, on board *Moa*, recalled the routine:

We would be doing a slow patrol about a mile or mile and a half off and sweep a big half circle from the shore outside and around and back slowly all day. Outside that again there was an American destroyer or two. It was very monotonous work. The weather was hot and sticky. At nights we were still doing this … although frequently we would be anchored and just keeping an anti-submarine Asdic watch … We would go across [to Tulagi] for stores and water, usually lay alongside one of the American support ships, they were like a depot ship, American yachts. The first one we had there was the Jamestown … a yacht belonging to one of the big American millionaires, a fantastic job and she was under camouflage nets in Tulagi. The next

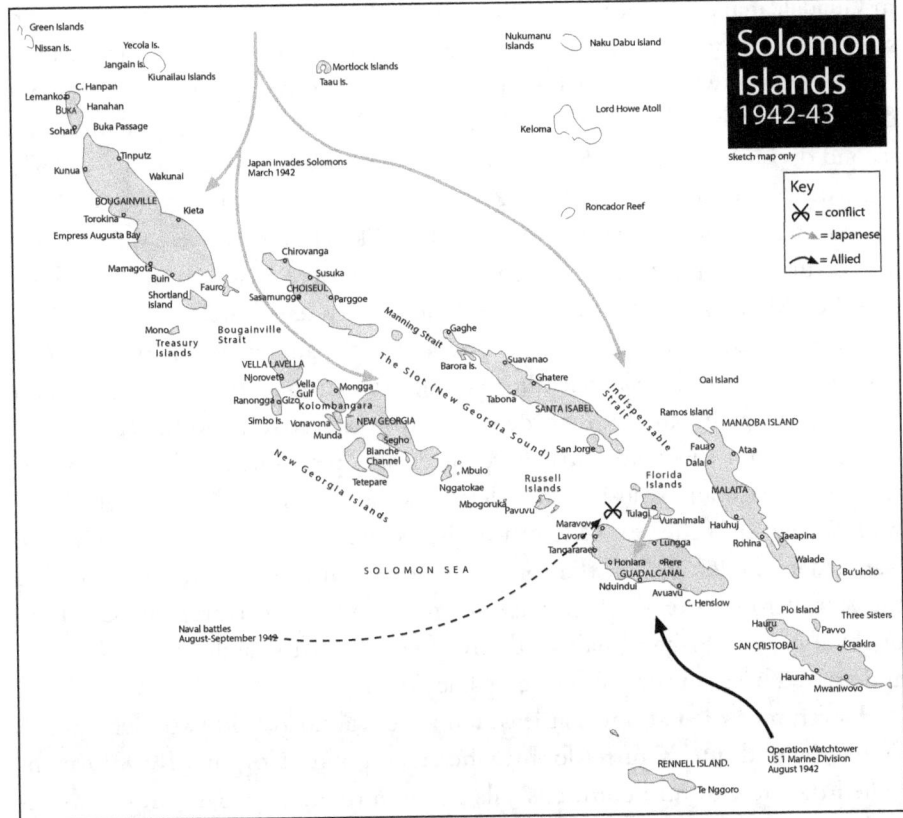

one was the Niagara ... belonged to Commodore Morgan ... from the New York Yacht Club.[100]

Japan was bringing supplies into Guadalcanal both by submarine, and packed into 44-gallon drums left to drift ashore. 'We would go up ... as soon as it was daylight,' Salter recalled. If they saw:

> ...any of these things floating we would fire at them ... We would pick up a few just to see what was in them, most of them were filled with rice, dried fish in amongst it and some ammunition, a lot of them were filled with fuel and if you hit them with a tracer, they would burn ... The Japs ashore must have been very frustrated, they did come out in landing barges hopefully to collect them before daylight, but I don't think they got an awful lot of stuff.[101]

Task Force 67 escorted a troop convoy carrying part of the US 25 Division to Guadalcanal at the beginning of January 1943. These waters were far from safe, and early on 5 January the force came under air attack just off the island. Allied fighters whittled the incoming Japanese down to just four Type 99 dive-bombers, but these pushed on and around 9.25 am hurtled down on the second division of the task force, which was led by USS *Honolulu* with *Achilles* immediately following. The New Zealand cruiser was at air-defence stations, with 4-inch AA guns and Oerlikons manned. Skeleton crews were waiting in B and X turrets, but at first the incoming Japanese were mistaken for 'friendlies' and their identity was discovered only when they opened fire.

Men rushed to action stations. The first three aircraft went for *Honolulu* and the fourth for *Achilles*, releasing a bomb from around 1500 feet.[102] Captain C.A.L. Mansergh had already ordered a turn to starboard, and the cruiser was swinging when the bomb struck X-turret and penetrated the roof armour, then burst with an explosion that shattered the gun-house.[103] The right-hand wall crashed into the sea. One officer, in charge of the midships 4-inch gun, watched as the left half of the roof 'sailed over our heads'.[104] It slammed into the starboard quarter-deck passage, complete with the turret-top Oerlikon pedestal. The right-hand half of the roof was 'blown straight up into the air and arrived back on the gunhouse upside down'.[105]

Eleven men died at once, at least ten were wounded, and two died later.[106] Smoke poured into X-turret lobby, where Temporary Corporal R.O. Osment rallied the crew to hurl cordite, shells and gun tubes overboard, 'rigged hoses and assisted the wounded'. Temporary Surgeon R.J. Walton took charge of the casualties.[107] There was no need to flood X-turret magazine, for which Kirkwood was relieved — 'having seen the magazine crew go down the hatch I don't think I could have lived with it … It would have been an awful decision had one had to do it…'.[108] The maintenance ship USS *Vestal* made temporary repairs at Espiritu Santo, and the cruiser sailed for Devonport where she was prepared for a journey to England and an early start to a planned modernisation.

Fighting around Guadalcanal showed no signs of letting up. The Japanese navy could not sustain the losses it had been taking and wanted to pull out; but army chiefs had assembled 50,000 men at Rabaul and hoped to push ahead on land. That essentially forced the navy's hand. However, the navy then gained full administrative control of the Solomons campaign in December, and Vice-Admiral Kusaka Jinichi took command of the South East Area Fleet based at Rabaul. He switched the focus to air defence, initiating new airfield construction further up the Solomons chain. On 4 January the decision was taken to evacuate Guadalcanal, but Japanese naval units continued to run supplies through the month, and New Zealand's minesweepers joined US forces trying to stop them. *Kiwi* was accidentally attacked by an American motorboat on the night of 14 January.

More serious encounters came during the night on 29 January when *Kiwi*, patrolling with *Moa* just off Kamimbo Bay, picked up the distinctive sounds of a submarine. Kiwi overran the target and dropped depth-charges. They lost Asdic contact on the next run, but after the third there was a swirl in the water and a huge submarine bubbled to the surface. It was the I-1. Although apparently unable to submerge, she appeared to be in little danger of sinking, and her crew promptly engaged the two New Zealand minesweepers with the deck gun. This was not a vain hope; the submarine was larger than the two minesweepers combined, and armed for surface action. As J.L.W. Salter recalled, 'They only wanted one of those bricks to finish us.' The shells screamed over *Moa* with a 'noise like an express going through a tunnel'.[109]

It was a moment for action. *Kiwi*'s bow-mounted 20-mm Oerlikon — an unauthorised addition 'liberated' from an American wreck — swept the submarine's deck, while Lieutenant-Commander Gordon Bridson ordered the helmsman to close and ram. *Kiwi* crashed into I-1 abaft the conning tower. The 4-inch gun continued to pound away at point-blank range, silencing the Japanese deck gun and raking the landing craft strapped to the deck. Bridson pulled clear and ran in again, colliding with I-1's stern. Again the minesweeper pulled away, and Bridson circled for a third attempt. This time Kiwi ran up on the deck and canted over, rupturing the Japanese boat's oil tanks and starting a small fire. By this time *Kiwi*'s 4-inch gun had overheated, so Bridson drew back to give Moa a clear field of fire. I-1 continued to move at about 12 knots, but was well down by the stern and the engagement became a chase punctuated with gunfire and frequent changes of course. Around 11.20 pm, the submarine ran on to a reef. *Moa* waited until dawn and as the light grew reopened fire with her machine guns. One man was rescued, but Japanese artillery ashore opened fire and the New Zealand ship had to depart.[110]

Kiwi needed repairs, and her place on the patrol line was taken by Tui. There was more activity next night, 30 January, when the New Zealand ships found Japanese landing craft near Cape Esperance. *Moa* was hit during the brief engagement, temporarily silencing her 4-inch gun, but *Tui* returned the fire and sank one of the landing craft. Two days later a Japanese force was spotted coming down the 'Slot' and Henderson Field came under heavy air assault; but the convoy was actually on its way to start the evacuation from Guadalcanal. This was completed on the night of 7–8 February, though isolated soldiers

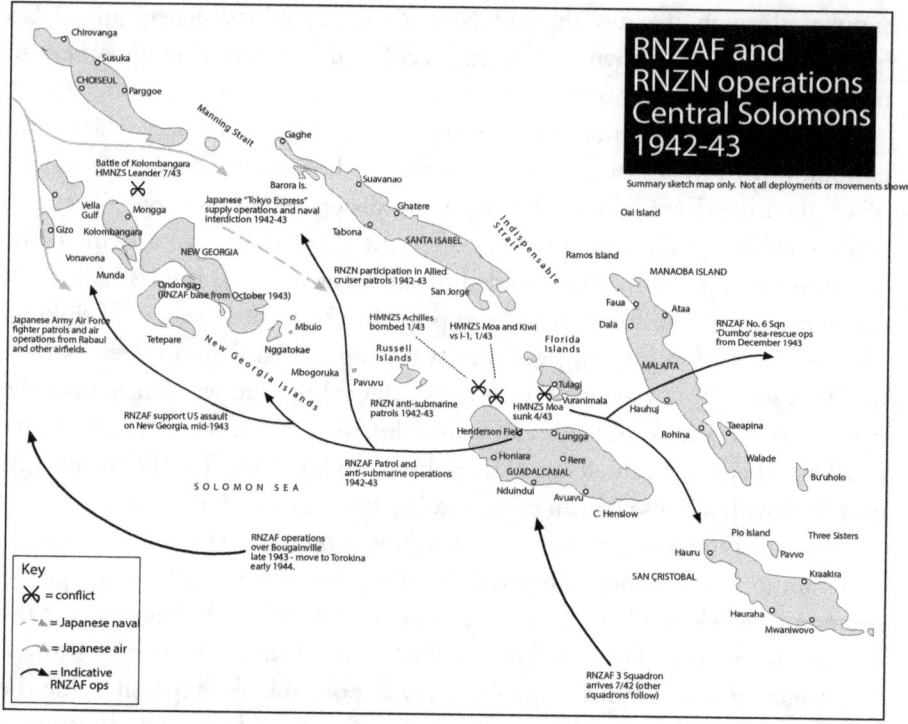

stayed back and made life hazardous for the Allied forces ashore. The struggle for the island had cost Japan 24 warships, 600 aircraft and 25,000 men — of whom 9000 died from disease. Japan abandoned Papua at the same time, and there was a lull as both sides sorted out their strategies.[111]

The pause between campaigns did not reduce the intensity of ongoing naval and air activity in the Solomons; the Japanese continued to push supplies through by destroyer and submarine, supporting the effort with regular air raids as far as Guadalcanal. *Moa* was New Zealand's next major casualty. She was detached from the 25th Minesweeping Flotilla on 6 April and sent to Tulagi to refuel and resupply. Next day the Japanese launched an air raid against nearby US forces, but when the American ships retired into a rain squall the Japanese turned to Tulagi, where *Moa* was fuelling from the oil barge *Erskine M. Phelps*. Neither *Moa* nor the oiler were warned, but both fired back as the aircraft appeared.

The Japanese scored two near misses on the minesweeper and a hit that crashed through the captain's cabin and burst below. *Moa* immediately took on a list towards the tanker, compounded by a heavy bow trim. Men hastened to lower the boats, but Leading Signalman J.L.W. Salter and Ordinary Telegraphist

W.G.T. Bright refused to leave an unconscious rating on the bridge, 'fitted him with a life jacket' and kept his head out of water after the ship sank. Phipps later remarked that they had 'undoubtedly saved the life of Signalman Thomas', and thought their action 'particularly praiseworthy in view of the fact that they had no knowledge of the side towards which Moa would list or capsize and sink'.[112]

Salter and Bright were recommended for the George Medal. *Moa* sank by the head in four minutes. There was time to lower the boat, but most of the men were left floating in the water. Lieutenant C. Belgrave 'dived for and sustained Assistant Stewart W. Molloy…'. Flotilla commanding officer Commander A.D. Holden was very admiring. 'This rating's life was undoubtedly saved by this officer.' The survivors assembled on Tulagi wharf. Five men died as *Moa* went down and 15 were injured, including *Moa*'s commander. Holden later reported that it was 'extremely fortunate that casualties were not more severe'.[113] Most of the injured were taken to the hospital at Espiritu Santo, except for Thomas who stayed on the critical list in Makambo for a week.[114] Meanwhile the salvage ship USS Ortolan tried to retrieve secret equipment, a task made all the more hazardous because the minesweeper lay in more than 130 feet (42 m) of water, 'and diving conditions are difficult'.[115]

Operation Cartwheel

The recapture of Guadalcanal eliminated any chance of Japan moving through to Fiji and Samoa, but the next Allied move in the Pacific was not clear. The Chiefs of Staff refused to allow MacArthur to attack Rabaul directly, instead opting early in 1943 for what was code-named Operation Cartwheel — a combined eight-month pincer attack on Rabaul through New Guinea and the Solomons respectively. Initial objectives were the northeastern coast of New Guinea, which would provide MacArthur's forces with a jumping-off point to the southern tip of New Britain; and Bougainville — where Halsey could bring pressure directly to bear against Rabaul from the east.[116]

Forces under Halsey included seven divisions, 1800 aircraft, six battleships and two aircraft carriers. The dual assault began with attacks on the Russell Islands in the Solomons and the Trobriand Islands near New Guinea. MacArthur then launched an overland assault on Lae, while Halsey began a drive northwest through the Solomons. The ultimate goal for the wider campaign, thought to be attainable within eight months, was the liberation of New Britain and Rabaul.

However, MacArthur's thrust through New Guinea soon bogged down. This did not bode well, particularly as he saw the drive to Rabaul as preliminary to a return to the Philippines. He campaigned intensively for the latter during early 1943, calling for a concentrated thrust along the New Guinea-Mindanao axis, ostensibly on the basis that the United States had lost face in Asia and needed to reassert itself militarily through the same area in order to regain influence. The plan was opposed by King and Nimitz, who preferred a naval campaign through the Gilbert, Marshall, Caroline and Marianas islands, directly to Japan. In May the Chiefs of Staff produced a compromise, backing both Nimitz and MacArthur on the argument that Japan could not block two thrusts. The real reason was political — Roosevelt was not prepared to compromise his earlier decision to split the Pacific command.

These issues were unresolved when US troops landed on New Georgia in June. Although initial resistance was light the Japanese garrison soon began putting up the customary opposition. The Americans had to pour another division and a half into the battle, and fighting continued into July. The war at sea again devolved to a struggle between Japanese forces running supplies into the island, and Allied squadrons trying to stop them. By this time *Leander*, now under Mansergh, was back in the Solomons after convoy duties into the Pacific. After some debate over her employment, fuelled by the fact that *Leander* had torpedo tubes and in theory could have joined US destroyers, she joined the cruiser-based Task Force 18.

On *Leander*'s second patrol, during the early hours of 13 July, the force ran into five destroyers and the cruiser *Jintsu* off Kolombangara. The Allied force worked up to 28 knots and swung in a sharp S-turn to close the range. As they did so *Jintsu* tried illuminating the battlefield with searchlights and became the target for the entire Allied squadron, which opened fire at a range of 11,000 yards. *Leander* joined in, ultimately loosing 160 rounds from her 6-inch guns, but was hampered by a faulty radar target bearing indicator, and when the searchlight went out had to use 'radar ranges and hits on enemy ships and his gunflashes as points of aim'. Visual spotting 'proved impossible throughout, due to the heavy smoke from *Honolulu*'s guns'.[117] At 1.14 am *Leander* fired torpedoes to starboard, and about the same time the destroyers *Yugure*, *Kiyonami*, *Hamakaze* and *Yukikaze* loosed their own salvoes of deadly Long Lance torpedoes, the fastest and most powerful 'tin fish' in the world. Two minutes later Admiral W.L. Ainsworth signalled a 180-degree turn to port. *Leander* did not receive the signal, nor did most of the rear destroyers, and one minute later her lookouts and bridge crew saw 'through a gap in the smoke that *Honolulu* had started to turn ... drastic avoiding action had to be taken and fire was checked after 21 broadsides'.

As *Leander* straightened to follow St Louis, a Long Lance slammed into the port side around Frame 87, abaft 'A' boiler room. There was a huge explosion, and a 'heavy column of water was thrown up', dousing the after part of the ship.[118] The cruiser had no effective anti-torpedo protection, and the devastation inside the cruiser was incredible. Six men died at once as the blast ripped a hole in the shell plating and roared through 'A' boiler room. Over-pressure vented through a fan duct and blew eight men overboard.[119] Fifteen more were badly wounded;[120] and many others received minor blows, cuts and shock as the blast jolted the ship from stem to stern, whipping the hull and sending equipment flying. Over-pressure distorted the hull 50 feet (16.5 m) fore and aft of the impact point and damaged the bottom plating to the turn of the bilge. The side above the hole was cracked. The stoker's messdeck above was smashed and the deckhead split. Most of the bulkheads in 'A' boiler room were strained or cracked. Five fuel tanks were wrecked, and two more contaminated with salt water. Water gushed into 'A' boiler room, spreading quickly to the main switchboard and No. 4 breaker spaces, the forward dynamo room, the 6-inch transmitting station and the No. 1 Low Power Room. 'B' boiler room fans failed, forcing the crew to evacuate. Men thrashed their way to safety through rising water in the darkness. Above decks a circuit breaker snapped shut on the after searchlight and the lamp flared out over the sea. A sailor slammed his hand through the searchlight hatch and broke the circuit, burning his arm but extinguishing the lamp. Steam failed to the after engines, and electrical power was cut off 'everywhere forwards of "C" boiler rooms'.[121]

It was a devastating blow, and with large below-water compartments swiftly flooding the ship quickly took on a ten-degree list. Commander Stephen W. Roskill, the Executive Officer, began co-ordinating damage control. He was a career Royal Navy officer, one of a number aboard the ship, and in many respects it was fortunate he was on board. Early Royal Navy experiences during the war had underscored significant lapses in their damage-control procedures. Correcting them rested as much on the officers and crew of any ship as on official Admiralty procedures; and Roskill was determined to make sure that no such problems struck *Leander*. He had consequently paid intense attention to detail, getting rid of flammables, ensuring all damage-control equipment was ready, and requiring the men to memorise locations, procedures and systems. He then spot-checked their knowledge, often stopping sailors when passing by to see if they knew how particular equipment worked, or checking their understanding of a procedure. Those who could not answer, or got it wrong, received the sharp edge of his tongue, something nobody was prepared to endure twice. The approach stood at odds with the slightly more relaxed New Zealand approach to authority, and he was intensely disliked on the back of it, gaining the nickname 'The Black Mamba' on the basis that you were only bitten by him once.

However now, as *Leander* slid to a halt in the darkness, that training paid off. The men knew exactly what to do, and saved the ship. It was still a struggle; she was at grave risk of sinking: *Orion* class cruisers were not meant to be able to survive the flooding of two boiler rooms, and that is what *Leander* now faced. efforts to establish flooding boundaries focused on 'B' boiler room where Stoker Petty Officer A. Fickling and Acting Leading Stoker (Temporary) John Halliday led a small party through darkness, heat and waist-deep water to plug holes in the bulkhead. Rifts in other bulkheads were plugged and shored by a party under Chief Shipwright A. Stewart, while Acting Chief Engine-Room Artificer Morris Buckley closed the main steam pipes in the partly flooded 'B' boiler room. 'They had to shut all sorts of feeds down,' Harvey recalled. 'They had to close off feed water and … steam inlets and outlets…'.[122] Two portable pumps were brought into the space to dewater it, though water continued to leak into the ship and by 1.53 am the radio room was abandoned with 18 inches of water on the floor.

First priority was moving. Two of the three boiler rooms were out of action, but the boilers in 'C' boiler room were undamaged, and although the feed water had been contaminated, the engineers cautiously fed steam to the engines. Leander began to slip through water, initially at seven knots and later 12. Damage control parties shored up the bulkheads in 'B' boiler room and the stokers' messdeck.

Destroyers and an aircraft relay escorted the crippled vessel back to Tulagi — as one sailor recalled, 'we had a fighter escort from Russell Island, supposedly RNZAF, over us patrolling and looking after us…'.[123] Tulagi was a risky refuge, but Mansergh thought the ship might be good for ocean passage 'in about ten days time'.[124] Eight officers volunteered to run a cement mixer, pouring concrete into boxing built against the bulkhead of 'B' boiler room, and the Americans also pitched in. 'They supplied us with all the equipment that we had lost during the action,' one sailor recalled. 'Their Chief Petty Officers … were in every case I saw, very very competent indeed.'[125]

Leander sailed with escort for Espiritu Santo on 21 July. Mansergh thought the outcome was a 'bitter disappointment to me and to everyone on board;

there was but a fleeting opportunity for the ship to demonstrate her weapon efficiency…' However, he was deeply admiring of the crew, adding '…the conduct and bearing of all hands during the action and during the trying passage back to harbour was a source of extreme pride and gratification…'[126] No trace was found of the men blown overboard, but they were not far from occupied islands and the possibility that they had become prisoners could not be ignored. It was September 1944 before the men were declared officially dead.[127]

Achilles was due to return to service in September 1943, but a catastrophic explosion during her refit delayed recommissioning until May 1944. This left New Zealand with no cruisers, and after discussion Britain offered the relatively new Colony-class light cruiser HMS *Gambia*. She did not serve in the Solomons, however. The initial terms of loan prevented her deployment to the islands, and by the time she was fully transferred to the RNZN, the machinations of war politics had left New Zealand on the sideline.[128]

As a result the weight of New Zealand's ongoing naval effort in the Solomons fell on the minesweepers. There was excitement in mid-August, when *Tui* — escorting a small convoy near Noumea — discovered the submarine I-17 and made three depth-charge runs. Despite assistance from a seaplane the submarine did not appear and *Tui* abandoned the hunt. The pilot signalled *Tui* to try again, and soon afterwards the aircraft spotted a column of smoke over the horizon — the burning submarine. *Tui* opened fire at 8000 yards around 5.15 pm, and although the range opened to over 10,000 yards within half an hour, the minesweeper scored a hit at 5.50 pm and another at 5.57 pm — creditable efforts for such extreme range with her 4-inch gun. American aircraft attacked the submarine with depth-charges and sank it, and *Tui* went in to pick up survivors. The 'kill' was shared.

A few months later *Tui* was in the firing line. Three Japanese torpedo-bombers flew under cover of darkness to attack American transports unloading at Lunga Point on Guadalcanal. *Tui* was patrolling the channel outside and became the first target — though the Japanese aviators overestimated the speed of the tiny minesweeper, and missed. All three New Zealand minesweepers worked hard during the last quarter of 1943 to escort supply convoys. They were reinforced in early 1944 by the dozen Fairmile launches that had been providing anti-submarine protection in New Zealand's main harbours.

Chapter Four

Guadalcanal to Green Island

Can't see old Tojo lasting very long up this way somehow. It is very different talk from the early days...
— Ted Skinner, Guadalcanal, 25 November 1943[1]

In mid-August 1943, after months of debate at staff and cabinet levels on both sides of the Atlantic, Allied strategies to win the war were finally hammered out at the Quadrant conference in Quebec. The terrible casualties inflicted on Allied forces in New Georgia and New Guinea prompted a decision to cancel Cartwheel. Rabaul would be isolated, but not reduced. MacArthur instead got the go-ahead to surge west to Hollandia and from there to the Philippines, while Nimitz was given the green light for his central Pacific thrust. The decision to pursue both strategies — without compromising the 'Germany first' policy — put considerable pressure on Allied resources, particularly landing craft, with the result that a British campaign in Burma was affected and Churchill's planned attack on Italy compromised.[2] Both Pacific campaigns were also delayed while additional forces were built up.[3]

The push through the Solomons was still required to cut Rabaul off, but island-by-island advances had become too expensive. Halsey instead adopted a leap-frog approach, bypassing Kolombangara and Choiseul in favour of immediate landings on Vella Lavella, followed by another on the Treasury

Islands. This would pave the way for a direct assault on Bougainville, the last island in the chain.

Vella Lavella and the Treasuries could be handled by brigade-strength forces, and Halsey hoped to use 3 NZ Division, which was ideally sized for the job. Barrowclough did not want to turn the opportunity down although, as he told Fraser, operations would split the division into three groups: 'one in Guadalcanal, one in Vella Lavella and one in the Treasury Islands'. He could 'see at once the burden this arrangement would place on my administrative machinery' but decided that 'the difficulties were not so insuperable' as to make him reject the offer.[4] The tactical risks of isolated brigade operations were not high; binary divisions and brigade groups were vulnerable in the North African desert and Italy;[5] but land warfare in the Pacific was naturally fragmented.

The division began moving to Guadalcanal in August and September. The island was 1000 miles (1600 km) north of New Caledonia, seven degrees south of the equator and far hotter. In January 1943, Morgan had found the place 'Hot & breathless, like an oven, and [a] peculiar smell around which is hard to place. Everyone looks pale & yellow from malaria … Very dusty…'.[6] The men of 3 NZ Division found things were much the same when they arrived eight months later. 'By next week we shall have tanks up for showers, thank goodness,' Ted Skinner wrote home in late November.[7] In a long letter home a fortnight later he added:

> *Am sitting on my cot with just a towel wrapped around me trying to keep cool … Had a shower cold for here, but at home we would call it warm. I used to go all day without water in N.C. without ever wanting it particularly, but here I can't get enough, however in time I suppose a man will get used to it. It's funny how the sun just browns you & doesn't burn or blister, but the tan doesn't last as long as our own.*[8]

Rain was as much a problem as heat. He had gone to an open-air cinema, but decided he 'will not be going again in a hurry, my mates wanted to stay or I would have left early. It simply poured all the time & the picture was one of those wild west things. As soon as it was over the rain seemed to stop.'[9] Everybody remarked on the downpours. Waterman compared the torrents to Wellington rain,[10] and one of the sailors on *Moa* recalled:

> *You would hear the roar of the rain coming half a mile away … and the next minute there would be [an] absolute downpour, you could hardly breathe, the air was so thick with water … and it got very very cold because the rain was from very*

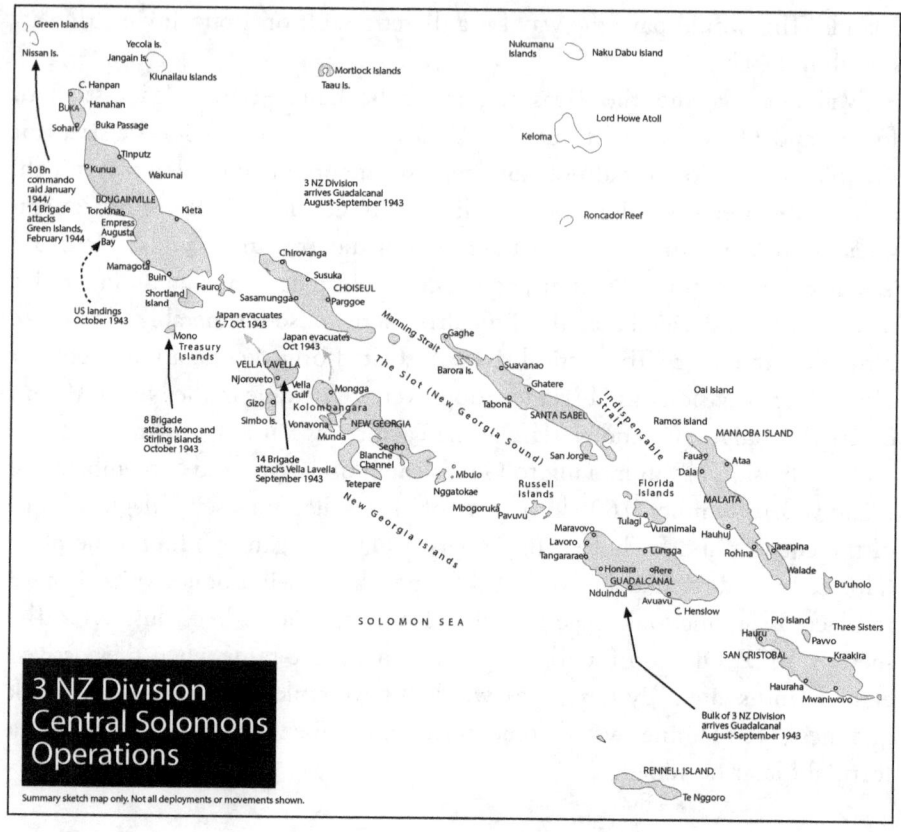

high thunder clouds, it was probably hail before it got down to a few thousand feet…'[11]

The sights compensated. 'There were fantastic sunsets up there. You would be watching a sunset, all the colours you could imagine, purples and blues and golds and reds and they would be changing all the time … and then it would suddenly disappear as the sun went below the horizon and then in about another 5 minutes it was dark again. I loved that place.'[12]

Guadalcanal was well into malaria territory, and precautions were enforced by a special Malaria Control Unit, initially under Major N.H. North.[13] Swamps and puddles — even tyre tracks — where mosquitoes were known to be carriers were 'sprayed frequently',[14] apparently with oil.[15] Some 15,000 mosquito nets were ordered,[16] the men were forbidden to wear shorts or roll their sleeves up, ordered to wear long-johns at night,[17] and were given insect repellent. They were also ordered to take half an atebrin tablet six days out of seven

— and a full one on Sundays.[18] All this prompted a good deal of grumbling. Many soldiers stripped to the waist when working in the heat, while barrack-room rumblings attributed various side-effects to the drug, including sterility. Others dismissed such talk. 'The officer has just been in to see that we take our medicine,' Ted Skinner wrote home. 'But it is hardly necessary, as only a fool wouldn't take them, but I suppose some are foolish enough not to.'[19]

In fact, many soldiers rejected the order, and as a result there were daily 'atebrin parades' where the men were given the little yellow tablets and ordered to take them on the spot.[20] It was draconian, but the measures paid off. Guadalcanal was thick with mosquitoes, it was impossible to avoid being bitten, and the same was true deeper into the Solomons. Yet malaria was virtually non-existent. Just 3.19 percent of the force contracted it during the whole Pacific campaign.[21]

Isolated Japanese soldiers still prowled the island, sniping and forcing the New Zealanders to patrol the supply dumps — they were 'told to shoot anyone walking round at night and ask questions later'.[22] Regular raids from Japanese air bases on Bougainville made sleep difficult. The tropical nights were filled with roving searchlights, howling sirens, and pounding anti-aircraft guns; and when alarm came, the men had to dive into narrow shelters hacked out of coral, often laced with sharp edges that could cut the unwary. Harry Waterman thought the foxholes were useful but added 'it is not nice to be woken up from a good night's sleep'.[23] These were not the only obstacles to slumber. 'At night the bush, which is fairly dense, is live with sounds; birds and insects keeping up a continual buzzing,' Ted Skinner wrote, 'bright fire-flies darting all over the place'.[24]

These sounds actually drew official attention. Barrowclough reported that the 'noises in the jungle at night have to be heard to be believed. Every conceivable kind of bird, insect and frog joins in a chorus immediately after nightfall…'.[25] As if this was not enough the Allied air effort went on continuously. Ted Skinner was impressed by the 'continual drone of planes' when he arrived in November to join the Field Maintenance Centre.[26]

The division settled into quarters near the Matanikau River, adjacent to the coast. Many units had a good view of the sea and the islands to the north, and some thought the place 'far prettier than N.C. [New Caledonia]'.[27] All around lay the relics of battle — 'plenty of old dumps [and] foxholes,'[28] smashed vehicles, aircraft, tanks, discarded munitions containers, and other detritus. Even wrecked ships were visible onshore. A good deal of 'dumped material' was still in good working order. Lance-Corporal T.L. Thomas' unit helped themselves to 'some small Jap picks and shovels' — at which point 'the stupid Yanks started dropping mortar bombs on us'. There were no casualties. They also found unexploded bombs 'everywhere' and 'have to keep a lookout for booby traps'. But the debris had a darker side, and Thomas soon discovered:

> *Lots of skeletons, equipment and ammunition ... Digging foxholes and digging up more skeletons, boots with feet still in them, equipment etc ... More skeletons, Japanese rifles, rations etc when clearing scrub. 31st. Levelling floor of tent today and three inches down found two American boots with feet in them. Gave up levelling.*[29]

Such revelations were sobering. 3 NZ Division had yet to see combat, but they were never far from the grisly realities of war.

Clearing Vella Lavella

> *On Vella Lavella, Green and Treasury islands the Kiwis ... went through the Japs like a hot knife through butter.*
> — Charlie Nicholson.[30]

The first real task that 3 NZ Division received was deceptively small: to help clear Vella Lavella. It was a rugged island about 25 miles (40 km) across, close to Kolombangara and clad in dense tropical jungle. The heights and beaches were separated by narrow strips of lowland. Japanese forces had landed in the northern part of the island to guard a barge station, part of the supply chain into the central Solomons; but they were not there in great strength, and Halsey hoped to take the island with ground forces and disrupt the supply line without too much difficulty.

The battle began in mid-August 1943 when US troops under Major-General O.W. Griswold landed without opposition at Biloa, on the southern tip of the island. A Construction Battalion — nicknamed 'seabee' — began building an airfield, despite Japanese efforts to interfere from the air, and an advance north to tackle Japanese ground units began in early September, pushing them back to a small area bounded by Warambari, Marquana and Timbala bays. The task of clearing this fell to the New Zealanders. A small advance party investigated in late August, while Barrowclough went over the plan with Rear-Admiral T.S. Wilkinson of Task Force 31, whose 20 amphibious ships were due to carry two 'combat teams' of 14 Brigade from Guadalcanal. Barrowclough

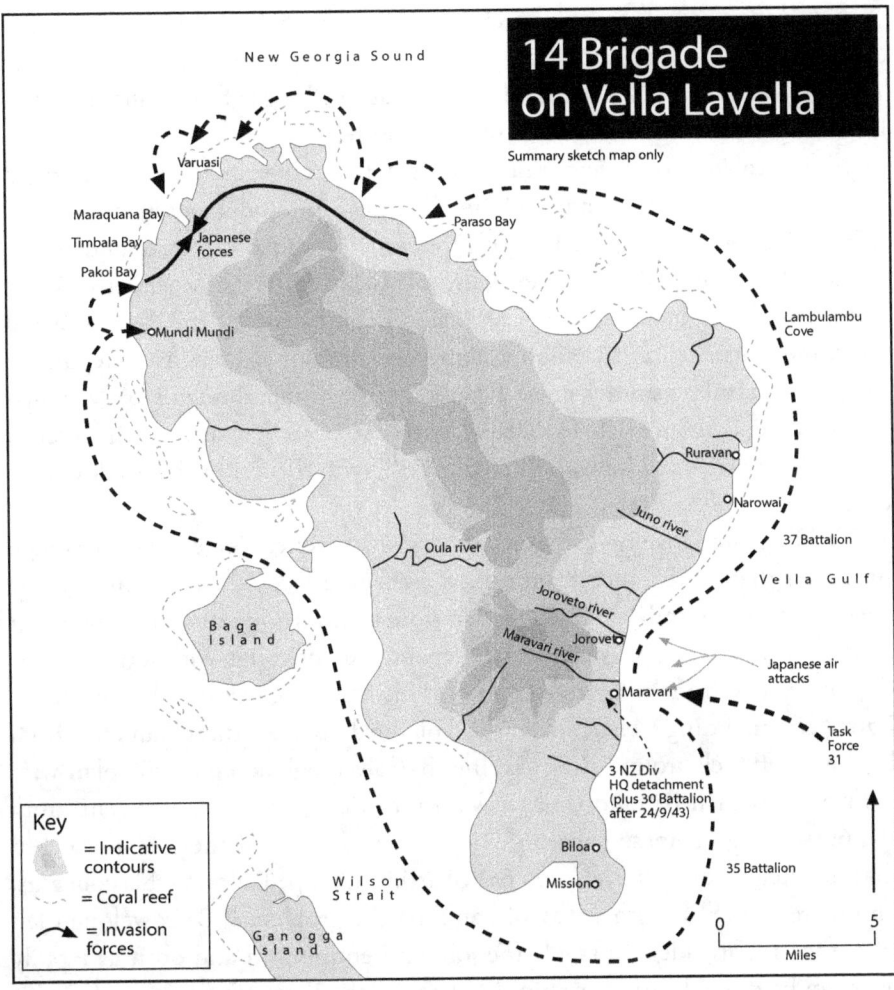

was 'somewhat apprehensive' about 'the possibility of enemy air intervention during unloading operations'.[31]

The convoy, with the New Zealanders on board, left Guadalcanal in the pre-dawn hours of 17 September. By first light on the 18th the little fleet was off Maravari, and the narrow beach was soon crammed with drums, crates, men, and bulldozers. They were sitting targets. Barrowclough's fear of air attack grew during the morning, but a 'small enemy force' did not arrive until noon, dropping a single bomb before coming under attack from the 'newly landed Bofors' and RNZAF Kittyhawks.[32] A 'spontaneous and rousing cheer went up' among the men on the beach as a Zero crashed in flames, a New Zealand fighter on its tail.[33]

Not everyone was on the beach. The men of 35 Battalion landed south of the rest of the force and tramped to join their fellows along a ribbon of 'stinking, clinging mud'. They had not been ashore long before seeing their first Japanese prisoner inside a barbed wire enclosure.[34]

New Zealand forces committed to the first wave included 35 and 37 Battalions, under Lieutenant-Colonel C.F. Seaward and Lieutenant-Colonel A.H.L. Sugden respectively. Part of Divisional Headquarters also landed that day, and Barrowclough took over the whole island from the Americans. Forces under command included a US regimental combat team, the New Zealand units, the construction battalion, an anti-aircraft and coast-defence regiment, a variety of naval personnel, and a Fijian scouting group, though Barrowclough hoped to send them back to Guadalcanal. He held 30 Battalion in reserve; they did not arrive at Maravari until the 24th, with the rest of the headquarters units.

Tackling the Japanese garrison posed several tactical issues. Barrowclough suggested that an advance by the New Zealanders could 'result only in the enemy's steady withdrawal before our troops and a long and perhaps never ending chase'.[35] This was an overstatement, but ongoing withdrawal in the face of a single-front advance was an obvious defensive tactic and Brigadier L. Potter, commanding 14 Brigade, instead planned a pincer attack, launched from landing craft well around the coastline. Barrowclough accepted the plan with reservations. Each battalion, alone, was numerically 'not very different' from the 600-strong Japanese garrison, and there was a risk of them being picked off separately. However, the 'presence of artillery' helped alleviate his concerns, and there seemed no other way of handling the problem.[36] Barrowclough felt 'sure that 14 Brigade will tackle the job with enthusiasm and do it as rapidly as it can be done, bearing in mind that this is the Brigade's first experience of actual combat.'[37]

Each battalion was organised as a self-contained 'combat team', with insect repellent, atebrin, chlorinating tablets, medical kits, American 'C' and 'K' rations, and virulent green jungle suits. These outfits were apparently far too hot for the tropics and came in only two sizes — 'too large and too small'. Kit included a waterproof poncho, toilet gear, eating utensils — 'and spare socks'. Webbing belts had room for the men to festoon themselves with everything from grenades to a water bottle.[38]

Advance parties moved around the island on 21 September, looking for landing sites. Barrowclough thought the Japanese were waiting for evacuation and would be 'prepared to defend' their little corner '"to the death"…'[39] Picked men from 35 Battalion circled west by sea to Mundi Mundi, a narrow beach backed by a coconut plantation. T.L. Thomas recalled that the weather broke when they landed and:

> *our troubles started. We did not know then where the Japs were, so we spent an uncomfortable night, just a handful of us with our backs to the sea, lying in holes with six inches of water ... Wednesday night we spent in a shed which had been used for storing copra ... it rained just like the previous night ... Thursday. Away at daylight, just 24 of us now as one man went back with dysentery yesterday. We marched through a swamp all morning, knee high in many places and ankle deep all the way to Matsuroto Bay [sic]. It was not quite so nerve-wracking as we contacted two natives who told us that the Japs were camped four miles along the coast. We spent the night on the other side of the Bay, which we crossed in a native canoe ... In the morning ... Two of our members went on ahead for two miles and saw four Japs in a listening post. In fact were only five yards from them ... Again it rained...* [40]

They set up camp at Matu Soroto and waited while the rest of the battalion came around. Despite an air attack on the 27th, the New Zealanders were ready to start the advance into Timbala Bay. The 28th dawned hot and wet, and began for Thomas around 6.30 am with the 'sound of heavy gunfire' as the 25-pounders shelled a suspected Japanese radio post on Utomi Island. The men struggled forward an hour later, forcing their way through thick jungle made all the more hazardous by torrential rain. C Company quickly found a bivouac. Thomas recalled 'bowls of rice still hot, cans of fish opened and half eaten'. The Japanese had 'flown to another unknown place', and the Kiwis 'had a good feed of Jap tinned fish and vegetables. The smell of their area was almost incredible. We could hardly breathe in it.'[41]

By 8.15 am, C Company had cleared Timbala Bay, and sent a platoon to find B Company, which was moving further inland. They made contact about an hour later, just as 'single shots and a few bursts ripped through the trees with an ominous cracking sound'.[42] One man was killed and two wounded — the first divisional casualties. A confused fire-fight developed in which both sides were hampered by terrain, foliage and rain. Grenades lodged in tree branches. Bullets whistled past with a flicker of leaves to betray their passage. B Company alone could not dislodge the invisible force ahead, and by the time A Company arrived the day was drawing to a close. They established a perimeter instead and dug four-man foxholes — rough pits that soon filled with water and slime.

A quarter of the men stayed awake. It was a difficult night, as the unofficial historian recalled: 'From a fitful sleep you could be awakened by the pressure of a hand on your foot. Then if was your turn … to peer through the inky blackness, and to listen to the disturbing noises of the night.'[43]

The next day began with another bombardment by the 25-pounders. The shells screamed over the leading New Zealanders, crashing into the jungle and tearing great swathes through the foliage; troops advancing a few minutes later compared the effects to a 'lawn mower'. Even so, C Company found a sniper. The three companies advanced in an arc, hoping to sweep up the Japanese ahead; but the next contact did not come until 11.15 am, when a 'strong pocket of Jap machine guns' held up A Company.[44] By the end of the day it was clear that the bulk of the garrison stood before the battalion, holding a neck of land between Timbala and Marquana bays. The New Zealanders slowed down to await 37 Battalion, which was advancing from the other direction; but the creeping advance took its toll. One of the soldiers, called to go forward on 4 November, suddenly had:

> …the queerest sensation, my heart seemed to stop beating for a minute, my stomach turned over and I felt quite sick. It took all the courage I had to start moving with the party. It was not til this happened that I realised the nervous state I was in after being fired on and living in such proximity to the fighting.[45]

Support took time to arrive. 37 Battalion had embarked for Paraso Bay on 21 September, but the advance party found the beach too small for the battalion to land. D Company was put ashore next day and moved up the coast, looking for a more suitable site. They found evidence of the Japanese ahead, located a landing site at Boro in Doveli Cove, and the rest of the battalion came ashore over the next few days. Movement was hampered by shortage of boats; the battalions had each been allocated eight landing craft, but this was barely sufficient, and the whole combat team was not established at Boro until the 27th. There was brief excitement that day when a patrol at Tambama Point, on the edge of the bay, captured a Japanese-manned coaster.

Dense jungle made movement difficult, and seaward hops to save most of the men from the trek were hampered by breakdowns. The movement was given impetus by fears that the Japanese might pull from Marquana back to Warambari Bay — it was 'essential … for us to get there first'.[46] Sugden was ordered to establish the battalion there by the 5th, and borrowed three landing craft from 35 Battalion to make up numbers.

Warambari Bay had not been fully reconnoitred, but a guide was on hand to show the battalion a good landing place, and C Company boats left Susu Bay around 11.15 am on a 'bright sunny morning' when the 'war seemed far away'. Thick jungle obscured the ground inland. They entered the bay, landed, and spread out. Fire-fights broke out as the beachhead was consolidated; the Japanese were actually withdrawing, but did not do so without a fight. Several men distinguished themselves during the next few hours, among them Lieutenant D.M. Shirley who was pinned down by heavy fire but nonetheless 'succeeded in flushing the enemy'.[47]

By this time 35 Battalion had advanced to the edge of Marquana Bay, pinning about 500 Japanese soldiers between the two forces. Potter ordered the advance, and by the end of the day on 6 October, elements of 35 Brigade had pushed through one abandoned Japanese bivouac and were on Mende Point. This compressed the Japanese into a relatively limited area on Maraziana Point, at the edge of Warambari Bay. The artillery of both battalions was readied for a softening-up attack that night; but the bombardment was truncated by the sudden appearance of low-flying Japanese aircraft. Late in the evening the men heard sounds of barges scraping on coral, and a short, sharp naval battle brewed out in the gulf. Next morning, Potter ordered the battalions forward. Lead elements of 35 Battalion made contact with their counterparts from 37 Battalion mid-morning and began combing the area, but found nothing other than the detritus of war. The Japanese had withdrawn under cover of darkness. Potter officially declared the operation over early on 9 October.

It had been the first real taste of combat for many of the men. New Zealand fatalities amounted to three officers and 28 other ranks. Two officers and 30 other ranks were wounded, and one man was missing.[48] Up to 300 Japanese soldiers were killed. Exactly what happened on the night of 6–7 October did not become clear until later. It turned out that a small force of fast transports, covered by six destroyers, had left Rabaul on 6 October and surged south for Vella Lavella. They were intercepted by three US destroyers after nightfall. The Americans got the worst of the encounter; and meanwhile, the transports went in and pulled 589 officers and men off the beach. The Japanese vessels then retired at speed for Buin, leaving the New Zealanders in possession of the field.[49]

'Now we took a look at ourselves,' one soldier wrote as the battle subsided. 'Most of the boys had skin troubles arising mainly from the lice … Everyone's nerves were incredibly [frayed] … jumping at any noise and snapping heads off on the slightest provocation.'[50] They settled down to garrison duties, building huts and making themselves comfortable. Even a field bakery was deployed. Barrowclough, meantime, flew back to Guadalcanal to organise the attack on the Treasuries, which was scheduled for 27 October.[51]

The Treasuries — Mono and Stirling Islands

> *The Japanese reaction ... was surprisingly supine. He completely abandoned his garrison to its fate...*
> — Major-General H.E. Barrowclough, 14 November 1943[52]

Defeat on Vella Lavella and the capture of Lae on 15 September by MacArthur's forces gave the Japanese Imperial General Staff pause to think. MacArthur now had an iron hold on New Guinea, while Halsey's island hop in the Solomons bypassed the garrison of Kolombangara, making nonsense of the blocking strategy Japan had adopted after the loss of Guadalcanal. New Japanese plans identified a 'zone of absolute national defence' which included the Carolines, Marianas, and South East Asia from the Dutch East Indies to Burma. Everything else would be held for six months only.

To hold the reduced empire, the Tojo government demanded vast increases in military production. However, Japan had never organised its economy effectively along war lines, nor implemented a convoy system. Despite early trouble with faulty torpedoes, US submarine depredations had whittled the Japanese merchant fleet down to the point where by late 1943 even existing demands could not be met. Iron ore imports to Japan that year, for instance, totalled just 169,000 tons — down from the three million tons imported in 1940. Coking coal was similarly affected, along with all other commodities, including oil. Food production plummeted, and by 1943 the daily ration had dropped to 1405 calories, generally below the level needed by an average adult for a hard day's labour.[53] Pre-war figures had been around 2000 calories, though even this compared poorly with the US daily intake of 3400 calories. Under these circumstances the increases demanded by the new plan were absurd. The shortfall in oil deliveries was particularly serious, because it carried immediate implications for military activity.

While these deliberations went on the New Zealanders prepared to attack the Treasury Islands. These were an essential preliminary to the attack on Bougainville, which was garrisoned with some 40,000 soldiers and 20,000 sailors, including forces evacuated from Kolombangara. The territory favoured the defenders. Most were stationed in the southeast, where other units on Shortland Island immediately to the south could provide prompt reinforcement. Halsey hoped to bypass them by landing at Empress Augusta Bay, and to do this he needed nearby airfields. Sites on Choiseul and Shortland were rejected in favour of the Treasuries. There was a site for an airstrip on Stirling Island, and Mono provided a good vantage point for early-warning radar sets — vital for successful operations over Bougainville. The third attraction was the deep-water anchorage in Blanche Harbour between the two islands, a 'good harbour for PT boats and small craft en route to Empress Augusta Bay'.[54]

The two islands were not strongly held by Japan, but Shortland Island — just 17 miles (30 km) to the north — was well manned with enough transports on hand to shift '3000 to 4000 lightly armed troops' to the Treasuries in a night.[55] That would be enough to tip the balance against the New Zealand brigade. Barrowclough's nearest reserves were 14 Brigade, 75 miles (130 km) distant on Vella Lavella; the rest of the division was 350 miles (550 km) away on Guadalcanal. Still, as he later put it, 'audacity often wins in a war', and he suggested to Fraser that 8 Brigade 'went on with their preparations quite undisturbed by any undue fears'.[56]

The assault, under Brigadier R.A. Row, was New Zealand's first opposed landing since Gallipoli, and landing craft were short — only minimum force could be put ashore in the first wave. Large ships were also restricted to Falamai, reducing any element of surprise. Brigade headquarters was expanded to help the planning process, but the entire effort was complicated by the need to deal with multiple US commands.[57] Preparations included risky pre-invasion reconnaissance led by Sergeant W.A. Cowan, and plans evolved into a two-battalion landing at Falamai, while a force under Major G.W. Logan landed at Soanotalu on the north coast to set up the radar station. Barrowclough wanted a battalion for that task, but there was insufficient shipping.[58] Meanwhile, 34 Battalion was scheduled to land on Stirling Island, which was not held in force; and 14 Brigade's 30 Battalion remained on Vella Lavella in reserve.

The operation was scheduled to match the US attack on Empress Augusta Bay, but early in October was advanced to the 27th. The brigade trained hard during the first weeks of the month, practising with a dozen landing craft on Florida Island. The slower elements left on the 23rd, and the rest followed over the next two days, staging via the Russell Islands and Rendova. Cowan's force went ahead by torpedo boat, landing during the night of the 26th to cut telephone lines. They also located RNZAF Warrant Officer G.I. Luoni, who had been hiding on Mono after being shot down some time earlier.[59]

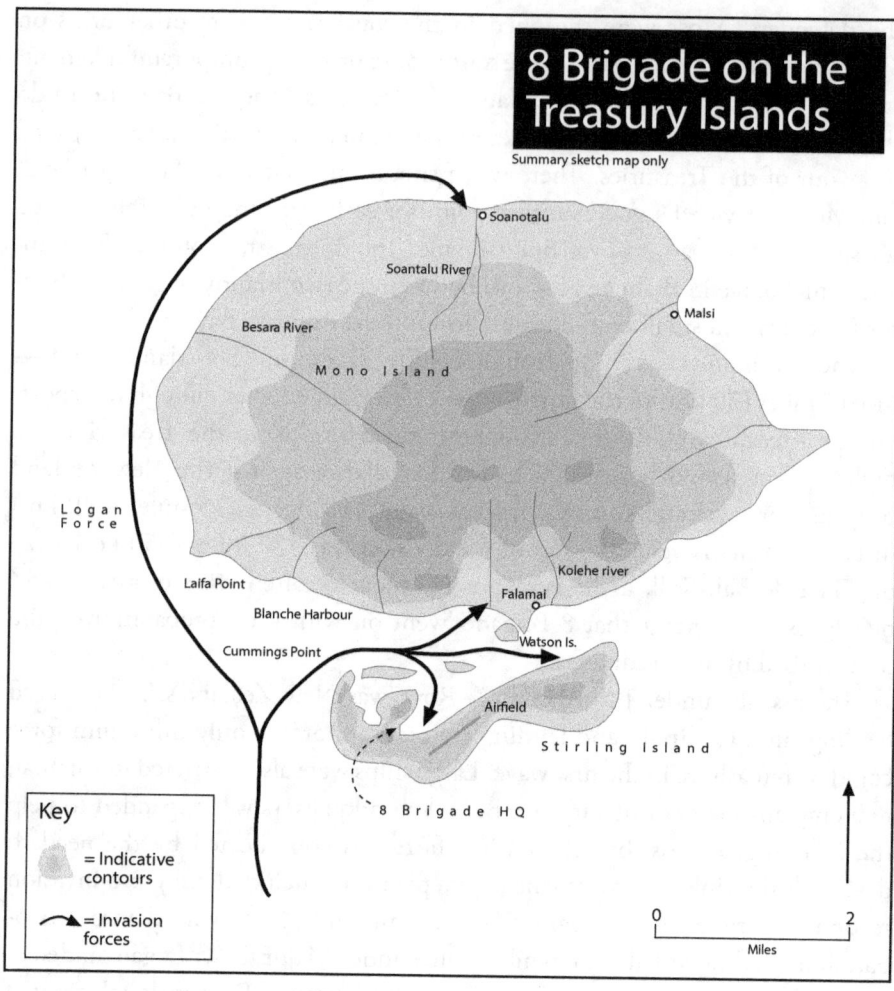

Darkness pressed close as the landing craft and destroyers neared Stirling Island in the early hours of the 27th. There was no moon, nor were stars visible under an overcast sky and 'even the troops on board seemed hushed in silence'.[60] The landings — scheduled for 6.06 am — were delayed 20 minutes because some of the APDs were late. Rain was falling by the time they were at the embarkation point, and in the grey pre-dawn light the men scurried down the sides of the bigger ships into the Higgins boats.

Kittyhawks of the RNZAF's 15 and 18 Squadrons, based at Ondonga, arrived over the beachhead at 5.40 am — the first of ten patrols during the day.[61] Five minutes later the Pringle and Philip opened fire on Falamai, driving some defenders 'into the jungle'.[62] The first boats reached the beach at 6.26

am, two minutes after the shelling lifted, and the men stormed ashore. Within minutes they had taken several positions and were fanning into the jungle near the Saveke River. A second wave arrived 30 minutes later, while a landing craft poured fire into the battlefield. The battle was still raging around the beach when the first LST rumbled in, and as the ramp dropped a Japanese machine gun post on the beach sprayed bullets into the ship. Kiwi forces tried to engage the strong-point, but for a moment it looked like the vessel might have to pull away. At that moment Carpenter's Mate 1st Class Aurillo Tassone drove a bulldozer down the ramp, and, with bullets pinging and sparking from the blade, crushed the machine gun post into the sand.[63]

Other LSTs were met with mortar and machine gun fire from positions uphill, all concealed by dense jungle, and the equipment accumulating on the beach came in for a pasting. Some of the heavy guns and vehicles were destroyed, and the chaos was compounded when ammunition began exploding. One of the LSTs finally withdrew from the conflagration and re-beached a little way along the coast. Fighting continued through the day, as the men advanced through the dripping foliage. By nightfall Falamai had been secured. The New Zealanders dug foxholes and settled in among the jungle insects, in rain that soon became a tropical downpour.

While these dramatic developments were played out, Logan's group of 200 — principally 34 Battalion D Company, with support from the MMG company and other detachments — landed on the north shore with no opposition. They made landfall on a tiny bush-clad beach, where the Soanotalu River ran into the sea and pushed patrols out to establish a perimeter. The engineers began laying a road to carry equipment for the two planned radar sites up the hill.

Stirling Island was also not held by the Japanese, although fire came from Cumming's Point, overlooking Blanche Harbour and Falamai. This was never sourced. It made no difference; by the end of the first day this island was in New Zealand hands, and the engineers began felling bush for the airfield.[64]

Everything had gone remarkably smoothly. Indeed, the Japanese seemed remarkably complacent; the Allied invasion force was seen approaching during the night of 26–27 September, and Zeroes tried to intervene over the beachhead during the day, but these were driven off by the RNZAF, and other support from Rabaul was lacking. Plans to sortie ten destroyers and the cruiser Nagara for a night bombardment of the New Zealand positions were abandoned. As a result the Mono garrison had to fend for themselves. Barrowclough expected them to head for the north shore, and 'harassed and hurried [them] on their way' with 'a series of aggressive and vigorous patrols...'[65] By the 29th the first

Japanese patrols had made contact with Logan Force, who Row reinforced with part of C Company. The newcomers were deployed around the second radar site, which was in operation by 31 October — in time, as planned, to cover the landings on Empress Augusta Bay.[66]

These deployments jammed the Japanese garrison between what Barrowclough called the 'hammer and the anvil'.[67] Desperate straits called for desperate action. The landing barge at the Soanotalu River mouth was an obvious way out, and a Japanese force estimated at 60 to 90 men tried to break through to it on the night of 1 November. The battle devolved to a brutal, personal struggle in pitch darkness. Several attackers managed to infiltrate as far as the barge, which was defended by its crew — six New Zealanders and three Americans, under Captain L.J. Kirk, armed with grenades and machine guns. Kirk was wounded twice during the ferocious fire-fight — the second time fatally. When his second-in-command also fell, command passed to the company cook; but the New Zealanders did not give up, and when dawn came the Japanese abandoned the assault. The attempt cost the Japanese 76 dead, 26 of whom were killed in or near the barge.

Two attempts were made to attack New Zealand positions on subsequent nights, but on nothing like the same scale. Row then had the whole island combed, and there were a number of short and sharp engagements. The last major group was flushed out at the end of the month, although isolated refugees continued to live on Mono for some time — including one audacious survivor who apparently made a home in the jungle within sight of an open-air cinema. New Zealand casualties totalled some 40 dead and 145 wounded.[68] These were the heaviest losses the division took during the campaign.

The waiting game

Monotonous days. Mornings work, afternoons poker, evenings 500. Sick of meat and veg stews.
— T.L. Thomas, late 1943[69]

I have never seen so much patience played as over here.
— Ted Skinner, January 1944[70]

The New Zealand efforts on Vella Lavella and the Treasuries laid the basis for the assault on Bougainville, and the US 3rd Marine Division under Major-

General Allen H. Turnage stormed ashore in Empress Augusta Bay on 1 November. The beach was held by about 300 Japanese soldiers, who put up solid opposition and foiled the effort to land on Torokina Point. The RNZAF was again overhead, and around 8.00 am Kittyhawks under Squadron Leader R.H. Balfour swooped to intercept more than 50 Japanese aircraft flying down the island. In the sudden, violent dogfight the Kiwis shot down seven, with one 'probable'.[71] The Japanese then tried to attack the beachhead with destroyers, without success but forcing the landing ships to move. Next morning the landing force came under air attack before fighter cover could be arranged. Halsey ordered raids against the airfields on the northern end of the Gazelle Peninsula, and into Simpson Harbour itself — Rabaul's deep-water anchorage. Resistance on land was less energetic, and the beachhead was reinforced and deepened. Work began on an airstrip at Torokina, and the RNZAF — operating from Ondonga — took part in regular fighter sweeps over the island during December.

This action bypassed 3 NZ Division. Barrowclough inherited administrative responsibility for his area, a task that involved a good deal of donkey-work, including manhandling petrol drums, foodstuffs and other supplies to feed the US war machine, but outside this the men had nothing to do. Training could only soak up so much time. Official visits offered one break from routine. The Governor-General of New Zealand, Sir Cyril Newall, visited Vella Lavella during November to hand out decorations. Halsey swept by the same month. Movies offered another diversion, though the rainy season made the outdoor venues a gamble. 'We leave early to get a seat and sit for an hour and a half waiting,' Ted Skinner wrote 'at starting time we nearly always get a fairly heavy shower.'[72] The rain also made laundry difficult to dry. 'Two glorious days of sunshine,' he wrote later 'in which we got things dry, but it poured down yesterday afternoon & last night.'[73] They were often confined to their tents by the downpours, adding to the monotony.[74]

The concert party made a welcome appearance in November, reaching Vella Lavella on the 13th to offer its 'first concert since Necal [New Caledonia] days ... delightful entertainment'.[75] Some soldiers whittled jewellery and nick-nacks from local materials or war debris. This practice was so widespread on Vella Lavella that 14 Brigade ran an exhibition of 294 items ranging from sea-shell jewellery to 'woodwork articles' that were 'as good as any' in New Zealand shops.[76] One of the 35 Battalion companies built model boats. On the Treasuries, bored 8 Brigade soldiers amused themselves running yacht races on Blanche Harbour.

By December most of the New Zealanders were looking forward to Christmas. An earthquake shattered the dawn peace on Vella Lavella on 24 December, giving the men a 'free ride on our stretchers',[77] and for a while there was concern about tidal waves. The sea had settled by afternoon when festivities opened with a swimming carnival. However, the 'whole success' of the festive season, as the 30 Battalion unofficial history put it, 'depended on one thing'.[78] Beer. Seven bottles per man — five for Christmas with, in theory, two more reserved for New Year. When combined with home-brewed and highly alcoholic 'jungle juice', the result was a 'bright and cheerful' evening.[79]

Special efforts were made to cater for this fourth Christmas of the war. In earlier years the men had been given little more than the standard rations, but by 1943 fare included turkey with cranberry sauce — courtesy of the US logistics train — roast potatoes, pumpkin and green peas.[80] Next day the men began a week-long athletics competition, though there were always reminders of the war. The men on Mono ran, hurdled and swam against a backdrop of burning airfields on Shortland Island.

Commando raid on Nissan Island

Either Island of course involves our stretching out our necks to uncomfortably close proximity to strong Japanese forces on New Ireland and we have behind us very large Japanese forces in Choiseul, Bougainville and Buka islands.
— Major-General Harold Barrowclough, 6 January 1944[81]

By early 1944, fighters operating from Torokina — including RNZAF Kittyhawks — could escort bombers all the way to Rabaul. The battle for Bougainville had yet to begin in earnest, but with the airfield secured Halsey did not need to conquer the island before closing the ring around New Britain. There was some urgency. Nimitz's central Pacific thrust began in November with a 'bloody, costly, ghastly'[82] assault on Tarawa. Forces hurled ashore in the brutal battle for the island included US forces previously based in New Zealand. Against these developments the Solomons-New Britain campaign had to be kept on schedule to secure Nimitz's southern flank and allow MacArthur to re-focus on the Philippines.

The next shore target was Kavieng, on the northwestern tip of New Ireland, needed to finally isolate Rabaul, and the United States needed advanced air bases for these operations. At a conference just before Christmas 1943, MacArthur plumped for the Green Island Group, just 117 miles (180 km) from Rabaul and conveniently within range of Torokina-based aircraft. Wilkinson preferred Boang Island, to the northwest, or Borpop on New Ireland. However, both were out of range of land-based air support from Torokina, and the balance was tipped by Halsey's additional requirement for an MTB base across the Japanese supply route to Bougainville. He ordered Wilkinson to take the Green Islands, a trio of islands encompassing a pleasant lagoon. Nissan, the largest — also known informally as 'Green Island' — included a good site for an airstrip.

It was called Operation Squarepeg, and the New Zealanders got the job. Wilkinson gave Barrowclough advance warning on 31 December with a tentative date in late January; but 'almost immediately the date was altered to the 1st Feb'. This was short notice, and Barrowclough was 'compelled' to 'move a good part' of his headquarters to Guadalcanal 'where I can be in touch with Admiral Wilkinson'.[83] He was then advised that the primary attack would be delayed to 15 February, but it was another fortnight before Halsey confirmed the arrangement, adding instructions to have a fighter strip completed by 20 March.

The attack put the Kiwis ahead of the front line with 'very large Japanese forces in Choiseul, Bougainville and Buka Islands' behind them. This carried risks, and although 'Navy and Air' were 'confident that they can prevent a considerable counter attack', Barrowclough still wanted 'to be as strong ... as it is humanly possible to be', and suggested adding tanks to the brigade group.[84] The other problem was information. Aerial photographs did not give enough detail about conditions on the ground, and as the locals were thought to be Japanese sympathisers, Halsey asked the New Zealanders to undertake a reconnaissance in force — essentially a commando raid. Barrowclough picked 30 Battalion, under Lieutenant-Colonel F.C. Cornwall, '...which has not yet had battle experience'.[85]

Two patrol torpedo boats took soundings in the lagoon entrance on 10 January ready for the raid. Meanwhile Barrowclough assembled a 'very efficient planning and control staff' to 'break the back' of 'most of our loading problems'. He could not use the divisional staff because they had to 'move forward with the Division'.[86] Logistic planning was a highly complex task; supplies were needed not only for the 4,242 New Zealanders and 1,564 Americans tasked with the invasion, but also for some 1,500 locals. Stores — including 2000 tons of fresh water — had to be loaded in such a way that the right equipment was to hand precisely when demanded by the assault timetable. All this was soluble, but it took time.[87]

The battalion, as yet to see action in the war, practised landing on Mumia beach towards the end of January. It was very much a venture into the unknown; even the likely intensity of opposition was unclear. The New Zealanders left Vella Lavella for Nissan at dawn on 30 January aboard three APDs, escorted by four destroyers and patrol torpedo (PT) boats. They stopped briefly in Empress Augusta Bay to rendezvous with two PT boats. One of the destroyers stayed behind; the rest of the force arrived off Nissan and Barahun Islands at midnight, and the men transferred to a dozen landing craft in pitch dark, amid rising seas.

Inside the lagoon it was calmer, and the barges followed a PT boat to the Pokonian Plantation, grounding on the coral sand with a noise 'like sandpaper on wood'. The men surged ashore and set up defensive positions, digging foxholes quietly but with frantic haste, the shovels 'slipping through the sandy soil with a sound like ripping silk'.[88] Dawn came, and with it undisguised curiosity at the tropical isle. In other days it would have been paradise with its coral sands that squeaked underfoot, creating a ribbon of white separating the plantation from the azure waters of the lagoon. But there was no time to sight-see. The reconnaissance parties were on their way before 7.00 am, looking for landing sites, counting the locals, and seeking information about the Japanese garrison. Other groups, mainly from D Company, went across the lagoon to investigate the Tangalan Plantation.

There was no sign of the garrison, but the calm was deceptive. Late in the morning three landing craft with a mixed US and New Zealand group under US commander J. MacDonald Smith went in search of landing sites for the LSTs. They found the mission station at the south end of the island, which was deserted, and were returning to the Pokonian Plantation when Smith thought he saw a camouflaged barge inshore. He moved the little flotilla in to have a look, and as they ran ashore into a bay backed by coral cliffs, 'all hell broke loose'.[89] Two Japanese barges were expertly hidden nearby, and their crews — concealed in foxholes ashore — poured automatic fire into the New Zealand boat as it crunched up to the beach. Everybody forward of the motor was hit by the sudden fusilade. The rest ducked for cover, but Private J.H. Jefferis stood and loosed 15 rounds from his rifle — earning the Military Medal. The coxswain lay dead, and Smith crawled back to take the wheel. The war correspondent on board saw:

> ...Another murderous burst from the machine gun ... cut down one of the overhanging branches and covered the stern half of the boat. Through this two of

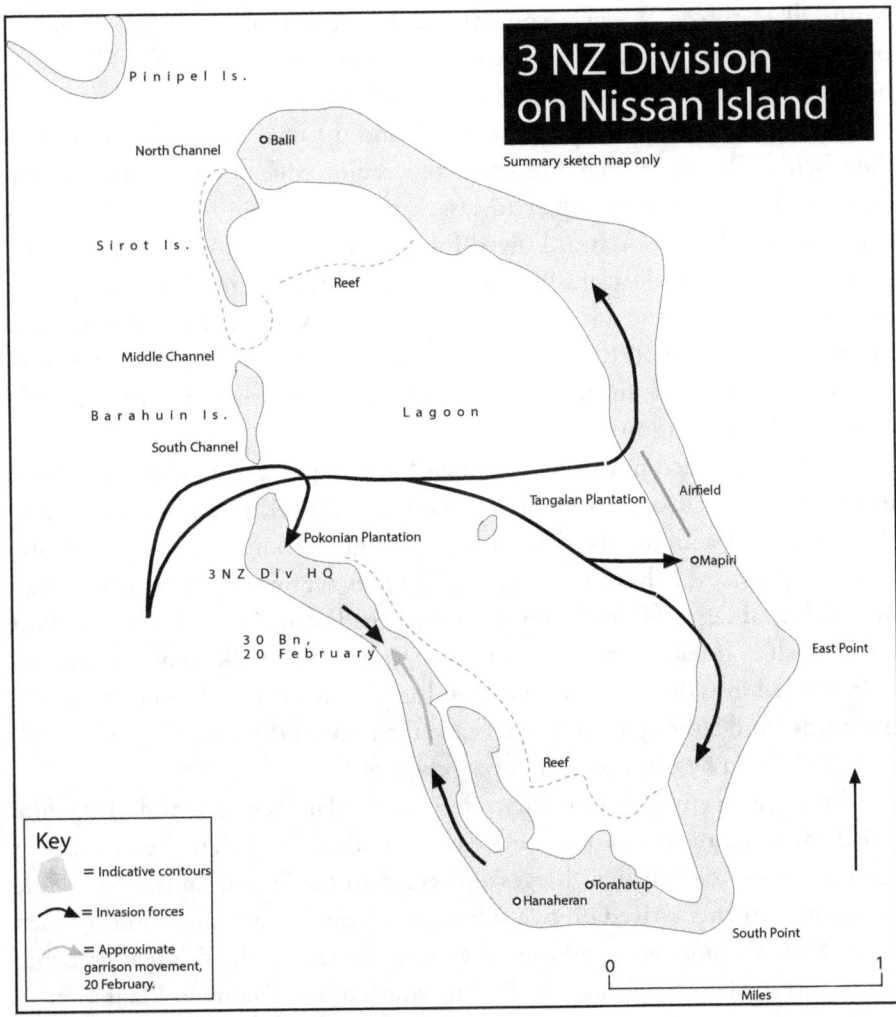

the New Zealanders, with as much guts as I ever hope to see, were pouring fire from their tommy guns back into the inferno.[90]

The two other boats opened fire to cover the retreat. Three Americans were killed and three New Zealanders wounded; one, Lieutenant Patrick O'Dowd, died later that afternoon.[91]

During the day, an RNZAF Ventura flew over and dropped a roll of toilet paper. Nobody realised that the roll carried a message inside, warning of an air attack.[92] This omission caused near-disaster later in the afternoon when the Japanese garrison finally brought the battalion under heavy mortar fire.

85

Cornwall scrabbled to get a counter-attack under way, sending one of the platoons overland backed with their own mortars, while part of A Company boarded Smith's barges to flank the attackers from the sea.

The barges were approaching the beach and the men on board had opened fire when six Zeroes howled into sight, 'the leading edge of their wings spitting tracer bullets' as they swooped to attack the vulnerable boats.[93] The boats scattered, and W.T.A. Aylward dived for one of the pintle-mounted machine guns, leading a fusilade against the incoming aircraft. The other soldiers joined in, breaking up the attack and forcing the Zeroes off. It had been a tense moment. Aylward won the second Military Medal of the day for his action. Ted Skinner, who was in the boat with him, later remarked that he 'certainly deserved' the decoration.[94]

Cornwall decided not to risk his men further, and as the boats came back to Pokonian beach ordered an immediate withdrawal, intending to hide in the shelter of Barahun Island until the midnight pickup. They left in haste, leaving equipment behind — including Ted Skinner's mess gear, which he had dumped in order to fill his knapsack with grenades, and was unable to collect 'in the rush'.[95] It had been a dramatic close to the day's work. Tension ran high as they eased into the shelter of Barahun Island, but the next few hours proved uneventful and although rising seas made the transfer difficult, they were back on Vella Lavella by the afternoon of 1 February.[96]

The engagement had a salutary effect on the Japanese garrison. They first called for reinforcements, but next day — not realising that the attack had been a raid — took to their barges and sailed to the Feni Islands. Meanwhile the reinforcements arrived on two submarines from Rabaul, and some 77 men from Wada Company got ashore. They were joined by the original garrison, which returned on 5 February and set up south of the Pokonian Plantation.

Green Islands

> *Fortunately for us the Japs were a bit slow, or didn't expect us back so soon & hadn't done much to improve their defences, although according to one prisoner large reinforcements were expected.*
> — Ted Skinner, A Company, 30 Battalion[97]

The commando raid opened the way for the full-scale attack on Nissan Island. Barrowclough discussed the plan with Potter on 7 February. They intended to put 30 Battalion back into Pokonian Plantation, while 35 and 37 Battalions were given the Tangalan Plantation on the opposite side of the lagoon, where the LSTs would land heavy earth-moving machinery and radar units. Other forces included the tank squadron under Major R.J. Rutherford, divisional artillery under Brigadier Charles Duff, and the medical services unit under Colonel N.C. Speight.[98]

News of the attack could not be kept quiet. By the 20th rumours of an impending operation were 'flying thick and fast', and the men were 'being issued with all sorts of gear'.[99] The move began on 12 February, although the faster APDs did not leave Vella Lavella until the 14th. By dawn next morning the force was assembled off Nissan, under US carrier air cover — a necessary precaution this far forward. They were seen approaching, and Japanese aircraft from Rabaul tried to intervene. At 6.00 am the men began scrambling down the nets into the landing craft, and the first barges followed a minesweeper into the lagoon. There was no opposition, and by 8.00 am the RNZAF was on the job overhead, forming an umbrella which was kept up through the day. The larger landing craft came in as the first wave secured the beachhead, disgorging jeeps, trucks, guns, tractors, bulldozers, heavy equipment, distillation plants, tanks, petrol, water, rations and munitions.

Everything went like clockwork. 'In half an hour,' one soldier recalled, 'the bulldozers had a road in, the Bofors were readied for action and four Valentine tanks were on their way across the Island. At another beach the CB's had the road in and had started on the drome.'[100] By the end of the day a cable had been run across the lagoon, six miles of road formed, and the radar was operational. This detected a Japanese air raid after dark, but there was still no sign of the local garrison and next morning patrols began ranging further afield, led by the Valentines.

Locals reported a strong Japanese presence on Sirot late in the day, and a force based around 30 Battalion B Company was sent to clear them. They landed next morning, disturbing some of the islanders who were 'observed frantically paddling away ... in their canoes'.[101] When the New Zealanders came ashore they were told by 'a very frightened native' that there were no Japanese on the island,[102] but a platoon under Lieutenant E.G. Taylor soon ran into a small force. They skirmished for the next two hours, sometimes at close range, and Taylor lost five men. Three others were wounded. However, they killed 15 Japanese soldiers. The island was finally cleared by 8 Platoon, which relieved Taylor's battered unit.

By 18 February, Nissan Island had been searched as far as the mission station. 17 Field Regiment bombarded the mission area next morning, backed by mortar fire from 30 Battalion, and the advancing men found a 'lot of deserted machine guns and ammunition',[103] and rations. Some of the food was later handed over to the islanders.

Where the Japanese garrison had gone remained a mystery until the 20th, when patrols pushed north towards Pokonian Plantation, not realising they were driving the surviving garrison before them. As it happened a 30 Battalion patrol under Captain J.F.B. Stronach was moving south from Pokonian looking for a new site for Barrowclough's headquarters, and the garrison was pinned between the two small New Zealand forces in a thick patch of jungle. The Japanese opened fire, and Stronach called back to 30 Battalion for reinforcements. Cornwall despatched D Company and a mortar platoon under Major Arthur Bullen, along with a medical team who 'went out full tilt' but could 'find out nothing' when they arrived and were trapped 'behind a big flanged tree with mortar bombs bursting round us for half an hour'.[104] Two Valentines 'came charging in and around trying to get the tree snipers without much success'.[105] One of the tanks rescued Private R.C. Stannard, who had been lying low since before noon. Unfortunately, as Thomas recalled, Stannard 'fell off halfway home, and we went in and got him'.[106]

By this time it was late afternoon. Bullen had the tanks pulled back while he organised his men under cover of mortar bombs, and with about 30 minutes of daylight remaining set his units plunging forwards. The battle was brief, brutal and lethal. Fifty-one Japanese soldiers died under the barrage of grenade, mortar and automatic weapons fire. Eight tried to escape and were picked off by 16 Platoon. Five others successfully got away. One survivor killed himself before he could be taken prisoner. The New Zealanders lost three killed and seven wounded.[107] Some prisoners were taken, and interrogation began even before the battle ended:

> ...Russell [Orr], myself and Nissei interpreters ... interrogated captured and wounded Japanese in the course of dodging enemy grenade, mortar and machine gun fire (second hand Kiwi scrap iron sold to Japan in the ... New Zealand depression). I saw Japanese at the point of capture attempt hara-kiri ... by doubling up with grenades held into their stomachs — their grenades were nowhere as powerful as the Mills and some of the yellow monkeys only badly wounded themselves. They never attempted suicide after capture and during interrogation were quite happy to spend the rest of their days behind barb wire splitting coconuts and smoking Lucky Strike cigarettes.[108]

Three days later a force from 37 Battalion found 14 Japanese soldiers hiding on Pinipel Island. They refused to surrender, and four New Zealanders were wounded by grenades during the tussle that followed. Apart from a handful of refugees — one of whom was not found for three months — that ended the resistance.

The New Zealanders settled in. 'This is a much better island than the last,' Ted Skinner wrote home. 'We are camped in the bush by a lovely dry coral sand beach & although it is malarial the mossies do not bother us much.'[109] Prisoners were held on Pokonian beach, and Nicholson recalled that:

> *Many were badly wounded and well served by our R.A.P. My job was to … encourage the Navy fellers to talk about Jap boom defences which gave the Yanks a lot of trouble during the Gilbert Islands assault … In the morning I used to take the prisoners from the pens to the tide and help them to wash themselves and still question them. Our fellers tossed them ciggies without rancour, saying: 'Here, Tojo, have a smoke.*[110]

Later he took the captives to Guadalcanal on a US destroyer. The Americans were less forgiving than the New Zealanders and Nicholson had to play peacemaker. 'Being an interpreter of an Asiatic language,' he recalled later 'you develop certain diplomatic and discreet nuances not always understood by the Western mind and I had the added advantage of Int Corp training so I was able to keep the peace between friend and foe and an eye on sullen crew members…'.[111]

There was a good deal of work to do on Nissan Island. The airstrip had to be ready by 20 March, a tight deadline for a 'green fields' operation. Barrowclough had divisional headquarters moved to the old mission station in the south of Nissan Island. Reinforcements arrived at five day intervals, a necessary precaution against counter-attack; nearly 16,500 men finally landed on the island, along with more than 43,000 tons of equipment and supplies. There was even a sawmill near the Tangalan Plantation, run by 37 Field Park sawmill platoon with assistance from US forces.

The best ground for the airfield seemed to be in the middle of the Tangalan Plantation, a stand of coconut trees which had been let go some time earlier and was rife with secondary seedlings, vines and the detritus of neglect. It did not last long. The pressure was on to get the runway finished in time, and the job started as soon as the men were ashore, days before the island was fully secured. Bulldozers tore through the foliage, demolition teams blew nearby coral deposits apart to provide material for the runway, and work surged ahead around the clock.

Night fled before batteries of arc lamps that blazed with impunity under cover of Allied air superiority, illuminating the labouring men and machines. Even tropical rain did not slacken the effort. The rollers, trucks and tractors rumbled on, gulping 8000 gallons of fuel a day as they laboured with inhuman endurance, served by shifts of sweating men. There was a cost. 'Last night,' T.L. Thomas scribbled in his diary on 15 February, 'a Yank on a bulldozer working down at the Drome had his throat cut by a Jap. Doesn't make for good sleeping at night.'[112] However, the work paid off; the first emergency landing took place on 5 March. By the following day the airstrip was in operation for fighters, and shortly was long enough to handle the B-24 Liberators tasked with pounding Rabaul to dust.

MacArthur's forces — the 7th and 1st Marine Divisions — were already in southern New Britain and steadily moving up the peninsula in the face of hefty resistance. The Kiwi contribution went beyond the airstrip; some of the radar units deployed to the Green Island Group were of New Zealand manufacture, built by the Radio Development Laboratory of the DSIR and operated by New Zealanders.[113]

At the end of February the focus shifted to the Admiralty Islands, when the US 7th, 8th and 12th Cavalry Divisions landed on Los Negros and Manus, taking both in short order. Barrowclough received warning orders on 6 March to prepare 3 NZ Division for a ground attack on Kavieng in the northern tip of New Ireland, but Wilkinson's naval forces took Emirau late in March and the Kavieng expedition was abandoned. 'Seabees' began building airfields on Manus, Emirau and Talasea, closing the ring around Rabaul. The Bismarck Archipelago was dominated by the Allies, who had total air and sea superiority. Japanese forces remained on the ground from Bougainville to Rabaul, but they could be left to dwindle.

CHAPTER FIVE
Tides of War

New Zealand's long-expected manpower crisis was finally triggered by the 1943-44 mutton season. At the beginning of December, Nash asked Halsey to release the New Zealand garrisons of Tonga and Fiji, adding 'unless these men ... can be made available for employment in the freezing works before the peak of the season in January, it will not be possible to fulfil the commitments in respect of meat, either for the United States Forces in the Pacific, or for the urgent needs of the United Kingdom.'[1]

This was bottom-line material, and Halsey complied. The prognosis for the 1944–45 season was worse, and by early 1944 the New Zealand War Cabinet was faced with the choice Fraser had long expected. One of the two divisions would have to be disbanded to provide replacements for the other, and to release enough men to meet coming war production demands at home.

Hard choices

Deciding which division to disband was not a simple matter. The war cabinet had originally envisaged removing the Pacific force, but by early 1944 there was an argument for pulling 2 NZ Division out of Italy after the fall of Rome — then anticipated to be not far off.[2] Under this circumstance a single larger division might be fielded into the Pacific, but the decision was complicated by political issues, particularly the relationship between New Zealand's contribution to the war and any post-war settlements. Surviving correspondence suggests that the government was groping for reassurance that a reduction of the Pacific effort would not affect New Zealand's position. Nash went to see Halsey in Noumea at the end of December. He was away, but Rear-Admiral John Shafroth and other commanders outlined the Green Island operation,[3] and Nash went on to Washington where he penned a letter to Roosevelt. This made the issue very clear:

> *How can New Zealand best serve? (a) By maintaining and expanding its air forces? (b) By maintaining its present naval strength? (c) … its Division in Europe (d) … its forces in the Pacific zone? (e) By maintaining and if possible expanding its production of food supplies, particularly butter, cheese and meat?*[4]

Roosevelt was reluctant to make a personal judgement but — as Nash reported — thought it was 'better for us to be at the entry to Tokyo' and wondered whether a British division might be substituted for 2 NZ Division in Italy.[5] Both thought Churchill should be consulted; but he was convalescing at Marrakesh from pneumonia.[6] The issue was referred, at Roosevelt's suggestion, to the Combined Chiefs of Staff.[7] They felt the US Chiefs of Staff were better placed to advise. Nash also raised the matter with General Sir John Dill,[8] but was unable to get a 'firm recommendation', other than a response from the US Navy that the decision to move 2 NZ Division from Italy was a 'serious one' that could not be 'unfairly rushed'.[9] This was likely a reference to the shortage of transports.

As a result of this orgy of buck-passing the question was still in abeyance when the New Zealand Parliament met in February. Fraser finally received a report in March which noted that 2 NZ Division was embroiled in the 'great battle for Rome'. There was 'no possibility' of sending them home until it was over. However, land forces were not an immediate 'governing factor' in the Pacific and the US Chiefs of Staff felt that 3 NZ Division should be withdrawn. If New Zealand wanted to make a Pacific contribution, there would be 'ample scope' in 1945 for 'a New Zealand division' to be deployed in theatre.[10] The British Chiefs of Staff concurred, with the proviso that New Zealand forces in the 'South-West Pacific' should be considered a manpower source, and 3 NZ Division should not be withdrawn before Kavieng and Manus had been secured.[11]

Shortfalls in British food production threw greater pressure on New Zealand's pastoral output early in 1944. However, the prospect of disbanding 3 NZ Division to fill the labour gap was further complicated by fallout from the Canberra Pact. Events soon took a hand. Roosevelt, Churchill and Chiang

Kai-shek decided in late 1943 to strip Japan of its Pacific island territories after the war. Neither Australia nor New Zealand was included in the arrangement, setting the tone for bilateral talks in Canberra during January 1944. These culminated in the 'Australia and New Zealand Agreement' — usually known as the Canberra Pact[12] — an assertion of Australasian interests. US government officials interpreted three of the clauses as an effort to reduce post-war US influence in the Pacific.

In the abstract language of diplomacy, New Zealand's military contribution in the Pacific took on fresh import. This suggested that 2 NZ Division should be brought back; but men were needed for the 1944–45 production season by August and the division might wait months for a slot on the transports even if Rome fell at once. Nor was the decision clear-cut. 'Germany is still the chief enemy,' Puttick reported on 19 February.[13] A 'really big' effort might defeat Germany 'quickly', a point that was not true of Japan. In the end, he concluded, it would be 'much easier to use men of 3rd Division to reinforce 2nd Division than vice versa.'[14]

Fraser's cabinet compromised. 3 NZ Division would be reduced to a nucleus and withdrawn to New Caledonia. A dismayed Barrowclough wrote privately to Puttick that:

> *I fully appreciate the impending recall to industry of a very large number of men of this Division ... I have not ... anticipated that it was likely to be so soon as your letter seems to fore-shadow. ... As a member of a so-called democratic country I cannot help being interested in the ultimate decision as to whether our Army effort should be made in the war against Hitler or the war against Japan. To me it seems inevitable that we ought to be represented in the Pacific where our main interests lie.*[15]

These protests made no difference; Barrowclough was formally told on 7 March and flew back to New Zealand to sort out the details.[16] It was, as Fraser emphasised, purely an 'interim' plan, awaiting clarification of 2 NZ Division's role in Italy, and the 'question of whether the 3rd Division is to continue or to be completely liquidated' could not be decided until then.[17] The scheme, formally a 'controlled diversion of manpower', was designed to bring 11,000 men back to New Zealand: 7,000 by July, the rest by October, for return to industry at a rate of 2,000 per month. Some 4,900 were tipped for housing construction, railways, coal-mining and sawmilling industries; the rest were destined for farms, dairy factories and freezing works.[18]

Most of the men on the ground welcomed the opportunity and some wondered how they might reunite themselves with their families. By 12 April, Ted Skinner's unit were 'filling in manpower papers'.[19] The flood of applicants was remarkable. 'Out of 110 in this Coy,' T.L. Thomas wrote, 'only 12 didn't volunteer.' Although he had contracted a 'beaut dose' of malaria he was determined to go. 'Daren't report it or might miss the boat home.'[20] He reported sick only after he was on board.

This enthusiasm contrasted with the official description of the withdrawal as a 'slow and melancholy process'.[21] In late April some 1,850 men left the Green Island Group on the USS *Wharton* and, a few days later, 1,700 left the Treasuries. More followed. Barrowclough officially handed the Green Island Group over at the end of May. The residual force now became prey to army requests for men to reinforce 2 NZ Division, and there was a steady stream of transfers from the remaining cadres. Debate continued into the middle of the year. An idea to rebuild the Pacific force and leave a brigade in Europe was howled down at all army levels. Puttick was particularly vehement, and Freyberg too came down firmly against the scheme. 'I am nervous for the safety of small detached forces in battle.'[22] In Europe, individual brigades were vulnerable.[23]

There was further change of direction mid-year when King decided to restrict further Australasian operations in the Pacific. This directly affected the RNZAF and RNZN campaigns in the Solomons and New Britain, and Fraser went to Washington in late April to argue the point, talking to the Senate Foreign Relations Committee and arguing the case with King. The latter refused to budge, and the RNZAF was excluded from action 'west of longitude 159 east or north of equator'.[24] The War Cabinet decided to accept this as 'necessary in interests of British prestige in Pacific'. Nash reported that: 'King's views ... are personal to him and are due to his strong resentment to the clause 26 in the Canberra Agreement',[25] but after a final meeting on 23 May he had to admit that 'King ... has a complete case on the disposition of our forces.'[26]

In July, Halsey's successor Admiral J.H. Newton asked for the remainder of 3 NZ Division to leave New Caledonia, citing logistics problems in the face of an arriving American division.[27] Eschewing King's attitude, he told Barrowclough that 'Admirals Halsey and Nimitz would be delighted' to have them back if the division was reconstituted.[28] Barrowclough tried to get direction from the War Cabinet, but none was forthcoming, and some 6,000 men returned to Auckland in late August, leaving only a rear party tasked with cleaning up the 10,000 tons of stores and 2,805 vehicles remaining in New Caledonia.

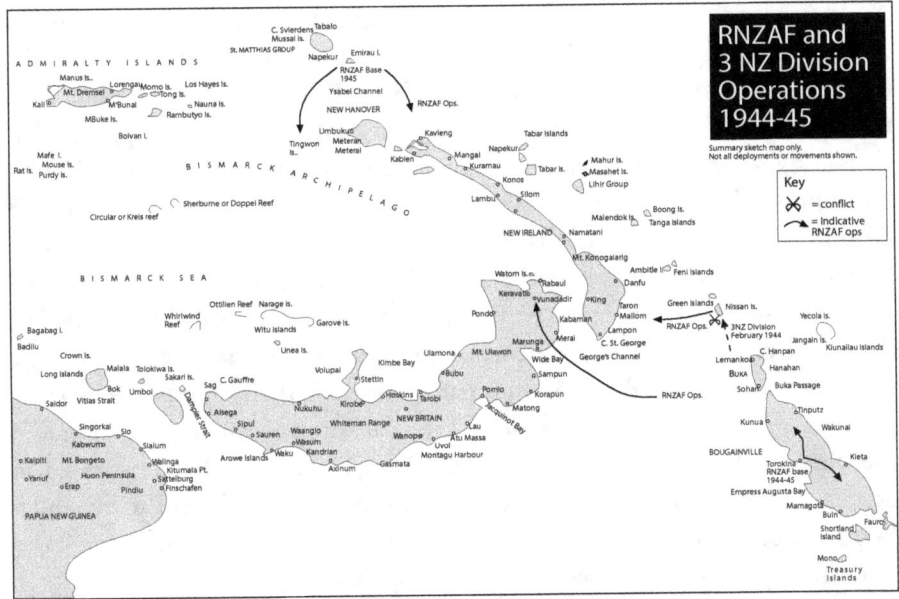

Barrowclough set up headquarters in the Auckland Civic Chambers and again tried to get direction from government. Fraser told him that even 'in the short period since I saw you' there had been 'developments which have necessitated a complete reorientation of views'.[29]

The main problem was that 2 NZ Division was exhausted, largely due to the fact that many of the men had been serving for up to four years, compounded by the two-month siege of Cassino in early 1944, during which the division faced some of the most intense and prolonged fighting of its war. Freyberg recommended replacing the longest serving men, effectively rebuilding the division anew; and the obvious source was the residual cadre of 3 NZ Division.[30] Barrowclough came to Wellington in early September to sort the issue out with the Controller of Manpower, H.L. Bockett, and Brigadier A.E. Conway — standing in for Puttick. Their report did not compromise. 2 NZ Division would stay in Italy until the war in Europe was won. After that New Zealand would field a division in the Pacific or South East Asia. Meanwhile, the two-brigade strong 3 NZ Division would be disbanded and the men not required for the New Zealand labour force would be incorporated into 2 NZ Division.[31] The War Cabinet approved the recommendations on 11 September,[32] and 3 NZ Division officially ceased to exist on 20 October.[33] Many of the men subsequently went to Europe and participated in the Buckland operations that brought the war in Italy to an end in early May 1945.[34]

These decisions did not prevent an ongoing New Zealand contribution to air and sea fighting in the Pacific. By late 1944 the struggle against the isolated garrisons in the Solomons and New Britain had been handed to the Australians, backed by the RNZAF. The service was re-equipping with Corsair fighter-bombers, Avenger torpedo-bombers and twin-engined Ventura medium bombers. These aircraft stood the Kiwi aviators in good stead, and 15 Squadron ranged as far as Choiseul. Three squadrons were based at the Nissan Island airstrip, helping to suppress Rabaul — aircraft were even put over the Japanese bases on Christmas day, though with 'negative results'.[35] On the last day of the year the New Zealanders put up three Rabaul patrols each 'with one doing a scramble alert dawn & dusk patrols one day then Dumbo the next'.[36]

These routines continued for months to a backdrop of official reorganisation; the New Zealand Air Task Force (ZEAIRTAF) was officially constituted in September 1944, to control all RNZAF units in the South West Pacific, under Group Captain Geoffrey Roberts. However, because of US prevarication it did not formally commence operations until July 1945.

Isitt visited Bougainville in March 1945 and reported that 'the mutual admiration and trust between the RNZAF and the Australian military forces would be hard to improve'.[37] The RNZAF's 14 Squadron was deployed to Bougainville on 2 April and began operations two days later with six searches of two aircraft each, 'the result being two beached canoes and a rowboat damaged by strafing'. Two days later, four aircraft under Flying Officer D.A. Corbett dropped eight 325-lb depth-charges on the road east of the Puriata River. Later the same day the strike was repeated with 14 500-lb 'daisy cutters' and two 325-lb depth charges. 'These strikes were successful,' the squadron operations book dryly noted, 'as the Australian Brigadier sent along a message of thanks.'[38] All available aircraft were put up on 26 April to support an advance down the Buin Road, southeast of Hiruhiru. The target area was 1000 yards long, and the RNZAF put the ordinance directly on target, which:

> *was devastated; some dead Japs were found and those alive in the vicinity were 'punch drunk'. Some Australian troops were forward of the indicated positions and an Australian Colonel, who had taken up a forward position, was knocked over by bomb blast ... some time later he said he thought close air support was very effective.*[39]

By the end of the month the squadron had flown nearly 900 hours. Some 10,592 sorties were eventually flown by the RNZAF against the Japanese on

Bougainville. It was a significant and creditable effort despite the fact that the location underscored the way that Britain and its Commonwealth had been largely sidelined from Pacific action by King's policy.

Last throw of the dice: the Philippines and the British Pacific Fleet

Although King had ruled the RNZAF out of direct employment in the western Pacific, New Zealand still had an opportunity to get involved via the Royal Navy. Churchill and Roosevelt took the decision to attack Japan through the Pacific at the Cairo conference in November 1943.[40] However, the prospect of British forces joining the US Third Fleet conflicted with King's intention of keeping the British in South East Asia and Burma, while the United States dealt with the Pacific alone — politically, a reflection of the practical secondary status Britain had in the alliance. This was where the parties came adrift. Churchill disliked the idea of a Burma campaign 'intensely', commenting that '… one could not choose a worse place for fighting the Japanese'.[41] However, Roosevelt wanted to cultivate China as a 'base for the support of our Pacific advances'.[42] Plans to attack either the Andaman Islands or the north of Sumatra were stifled by lack of landing ships. Admiral Lord Louis Mountbatten, in charge of the theatre, had to relinquish 15 LSTs and six LSIs in December 1943 so that the Anzio landings could go ahead without disrupting the Normandy schedule.

The strategy was subject to intense debate between Churchill and his Chiefs of Staff, and not resolved until mid-March when Roosevelt announced that the British were not needed in the Pacific unless the United States had 'unexpected bad luck'.[43] This gave Churchill the lever he needed to push a 'middle strategy', which included expanding Admiral Sir James Somerville's Eastern Fleet, which had been operating in the Indian Ocean since 1942. By early 1944 the British had nearly 150 ships based at Ceylon, including *Gambia*, now part of the Royal New Zealand Navy; and most were on hand when a portion of Japan's Combined Fleet suddenly turned up at Singapore. The Japanese had moved them to get the ships away from US air attack, but the possibility of a breakthrough into the Bay of Bengal could not be ignored.[44]

Around a hundred New Zealanders served with the Fleet Air Arm, among them R.F. Mackie of Waipukurau, who like most of his comrades made the most of sight-seeing opportunities while they were in Indian waters. 'I have just returned from a flying visit to Ceylon,' he wrote home in early May:

> *A very long & tiring journey there and back though quite an interesting one. This was my second visit to Colombo & although I was only there a very short time I took a great liking to the place. What a change too after being in the wilds. The monsoon is just about to break & it was raining when I woke yesterday morning. I just went and stood in it. The trees & beautiful gardens & lawns and everything was so fresh & clean. Colombo is one of the most pleasant places I have ever been to & I only wish I was living there.*[45]

These were valuable moments, snatched and held briefly between the terrors of combat. That month the British carriers — with *Gambia* among the escorts — attacked a Japanese naval concentration at Sourabaya. However, it was June before the cruiser came into direct action for the first time, when Somerville deployed four battleships, two carriers, seven cruisers and ten destroyers against Sabang. *Gambia* attacked the shore batteries, and the operation ended when the Dutch light cruiser *Tromp* entered the harbour, firing on shipping anchored inside. *Gambia* was joined in early October by *Achilles*, fresh from a major refit and modernisation undertaken in Britain. A crew exchange put ratings due for leave into *Gambia*; which sailed for Wellington, and *Achilles* took *Gambia*'s place in the Eastern Fleet.

By this time there was a drive in Japanese government circles to end the war. Rear-Admiral Takeo Takagi had concluded in February 1944 that, on the basis of Japan's industrial capability and capacity to import raw materials, victory was no longer possible and a compromise peace should be sought. The Cabinet Planning Board concurred, gaining the backing of the Jushin, the group of former Prime Ministers.

These pressures grew in June when the Fifth Fleet, under Spruance, attacked the Marianas. Admiral Toyoda Soemu, new Commander in Chief of the Combined Fleet, devised a plan by which the US forces would be pinned between land-based aircraft from Guam and a task force under Admiral Ozawa Jisaburo. However, the US force — which included 15 carriers deploying 950 aircraft — demolished the land-based half of Toyoda's air trap before it was ready. Ozawa attacked anyway on 19 June, losing 346 aircraft and three carriers in a futile effort to battle through the swirling Hellcats and intense anti-aircraft defences of the Fifth Fleet. The 'Great Marianas Turkey Shoot', as it was called, effectively destroyed the Japanese naval air arm, yet cost America just 130 aircraft and 76 aircrew.[46]

These military setbacks caused political ructions in Tokyo. Tojo and his cabinet resigned on 18 July as a direct consequence of the fall of Saipan, and

Marquis Kido instructed General Kuniaki Koiso to form a new government. This administration, however, fell almost completely under the spell of the 'hawks'.

The Americans pushed towards the Philippines. Landings were advanced to 20 October after the startling successes off the Marianas. This drew the fleet into the Battle of Leyte Gulf — the largest naval engagement in history. It was actually four related battles, in which the Japanese fleet attempted to stop the Sixth Army of Lieutenant-General Walter Krueger from landing on Samar and were opposed by the Fifth Fleet — now renamed the Third Fleet under Halsey. In many respects it was a one-sided affair. Japan lacked air power, and the first assault force under Vice-Admiral Kurita Takao was whittled down by US submarine and air attack. Strikes from the 11 fleet carriers under Admiral Mark Mischer sank the battleship *Musashi* and damaged the *Yamato* and older *Nagato*, causing Kurita to temporarily turn back.

A second force under Vice-Admiral Nishimura then tried to attack the landing craft via the Suragao Strait. His force was also whittled down on the way, and the survivors were intercepted in the early hours of 25 October by Task Force 77.2, which included six older battleships under Rear-Admiral J.B. Oldendorf. Nishimura ran into them around 3.45 am as he tried to debouch from the strait, only realising his plight when the old US battleship *West Virginia* — a survivor of Pearl Harbor, since rebuilt and modernised — opened fire with radar-guided salvoes, in the dark, at a range of 22,800 yards. The last battleship-to-battleship engagement in the world was over in half an hour. Nishimura's force was virtually annihilated. The Americans lost 39 men killed and 114 wounded.[47]

American material superiority carried the day, but Halsey's modern battleships were drawn off by reports of Ozawa's carriers to the north, and next morning Kurita's squadron erupted from the San Bernadino strait to attack Task Force 77.4.1, which was defended only by a small force of escort carriers under Rear-Admiral Thomas Sprague. In the running engagement, Sprague saved all but one of his ships and sank three Japanese cruisers. Nor could Kurita chase him very far; Oldendorf's battleships were waiting in the gulf.[48] Meanwhile, Mischer's aircraft sank Ozawa's carriers. This left the Americans free to continue landing, although it was Christmas before Leyte was secured, and June 1945 before Luzon fell.

The next major American target was Okinawa, largest of the Ryukyu Islands, which was wanted as an air base from which to launch raids against Japan itself. New Zealand was involved via the new British Pacific Fleet. The decision to form this force was taken in September 1944 at the second Quebec conference, against the opposition of King, who — as Admiral Sir Andrew Cunningham noted — 'seemed quite determined to keep the Royal Navy out of the Pacific'.[49] In the end King grudgingly agreed that the British could join in, conditional on supplying themselves. The fleet formed in late 1944 at Ceylon under Admiral Sir Bruce Fraser, operated briefly in the Indian Ocean, struck at Palembang at the end of January 1945, then deployed to Sydney.

In many respects the British Pacific Fleet was the 'main fleet' envisaged by pre-war policy; it comprised 100-odd warships, including all the Royal Navy's armoured fleet carriers, all the modern battleships — although not all served simultaneously — along with numerous cruisers, destroyers, and the inevitable 'fleet train' of oilers, supply vessels and auxiliaries. The fleet was also very much a Commonwealth force: RAN-manned destroyers and minesweepers, both RNZN cruisers and a Canadian cruiser featured in the order of battle. New Zealanders could also be found in some numbers on many of the British warships, notably with the Fleet Air Arm.

The fleet was based in Sydney, a logistics base was set up in Melbourne, and some of the docking facilities were provided by the Devonport naval base in Auckland.[50] *Gambia* joined in mid-February, and the fleet sailed in March for Seeadler Harbour on Manus Island, while the US Navy sorted out the political issues associated with their deployment. Finally the British got the go-ahead to join the attack on Okinawa. This massive assault, code-named Operation Iceberg, committed some 1213 allied ships to battle and was broadly a rehearsal for the expected later assault on Japan.

The British — whose armoured fleet carriers were better protected against kamikaze attacks than the thin-decked American vessels, albeit at the cost of aircraft capacity — were given the task of suppressing airfields in the Sakishima Gunto, south of Okinawa, and intercepting reinforcements from Formosa further west. New Zealanders serving with the Fleet Air Arm were heavily involved, among them Lieutenant (A) A.B. MacRae, who won the DSO for nursing a damaged fighter back to HMS *Indomitable*, despite serious leg injuries.[51]

Achilles was refitting at the time, but *Gambia* deployed with the Fourth Cruiser Squadron, beginning an unprecedented 62 days at sea. Japan responded to the attack on Okinawa with everything from bombers to kamikaze attacks — even sending the giant battleship *Yamato* on a one-way suicide mission. *Gambia* came to the rescue of the destroyer *Ulster*, damaged by a near-miss on 1 April, and towed her 760 miles to Leyte. It was a troubled journey. Ulster ran short of drinking water, which had to be passed in casks from the cruiser. Matters were not helped by a mumps epidemic on the New Zealand ship — at one stage there were 45 men on the sick list, and 37 were transferred to the hospital ship *Oxfordshire*.

Fighting continued in Okinawa through May. It was a busy time for the New Zealanders. On *Gambia*, things were:

> ...*happening all the time. There might be a yellow alarm ... the red used to come so quickly it was not funny. If an unidentified aircraft had got in past the picket or come straight in ... and it hadn't identified itself properly ... there would be a panic ...*[52]

On 4 May, *Gambia* and *Swiftsure* bombarded the airstrip at Nobara and, in 45 minutes, *Gambia* fired some 230 rounds of 6-inch at a range of around 18,000 yards.[53] There was drama a few days later when the fleet came under kamikaze attack. The Japanese had been hurling their young airmen sporadically at the British carriers for some days — without doing great damage — but the attack on 8 May was pressed home, and *Gambia* looked like a target. At the last minute the aircraft swerved and hit *Formidable*, causing serious damage.[54]

Gambia steamed some 10,684 miles during May, replenished — like the rest of the fleet — by the oilers and stores ships of the fleet train. In June the fleet returned to Sydney to refit, though not all the Kiwis had a respite; *Achilles* sortied that month with Task Force 111.2 to bombard Truk as part of a mopping up exercise. Other New Zealanders in the detachment included Fleet Air Arm pilots Peter Dixon and David Graham, both serving on the new armoured fleet carrier *Implacable*. With other cruisers *Achilles* hammered a seaplane base on Dublon island, expending 180 rounds of 6-inch, and engaging two Japanese aircraft with her 4-inch anti-aircraft guns.

The British Pacific Fleet — dubbed Task Force 37 to fit the American command structure — sailed again on 28 June to join the US assault on Japan. They reached Manus on 4 July to find the harbour 'jammed full of ships'. *Achilles* joined, and the fleet went on to Japanese waters where they meeting the Americans in a refuelling zone. The sea was covered with warships. R.B. Harvey, on *Gambia*, recalled that 'the further we went the more ships we would bump into, it was absolutely amazing'.[55]

Operating off the Japanese coast was nonetheless risky. Japan still had several thousand aircraft to hand, more than enough to overwhelm carrier-borne fighter defences. But they did not emerge. R.F. Mackie, serving with the Fleet Air Arm, found the 'attitude of the enemy ... difficult to understand — he refuses to come up and fight'.[56] Still, the relative lack of opposition gave hope. 'Perhaps it will all be over sooner than we expect,' he wrote on 20 July. 'I only hope it is as I am very tired of it all. From here we cannot tell so we must keep our noses to the grindstone and force on.'[57]

In fact the aircraft were being conserved to face the expected Allied invasion, and attacks were sporadic — though as another New Zealander put it, there were still 'quite enough to make a bit of a hole in the various Fleets'.[58] Mackie and other Kiwi pilots working with the Fleet Air Arm took part in a huge assault against Japanese naval bases on 24 July, which broadly destroyed what remained of the Imperial Japanese Navy. Airfields were also targeted. Operations were made all the more difficult by seas that whipped up to storm conditions, as one of *Gambia's* crew recalled:

> ...we would steam in towards the Japanese Coast, just out of sight a bit for a couple of days and aircraft attacks would be carried out all the day during the daylight hours. At night the heavier ships ... would go in and shell the shore installations and come back again before daylight ... That would be for two days continuous, and [then we] went back to sea again to meet the fleet train for fresh ammunition, stores, water, fuel ... We were delayed there with the hurricane ... we steamed around it for about three days ... The cruisers could ride over [the swell] ... if end-on ...[59]

At the end of July the Kiwi cruisers were joined by HMNZS *Arbutus*, under Lieutenant Nigel Blair. The little corvette had been refitted as a radar maintenance vessel, sent into the war zone, and made contact with *Gambia* and *Achilles* in the fleet refuelling area — much to the surprise of the men on the cruisers. On 9 August *Gambia* joined a small force sent to bombard the steel works at Kamaishi. The cannonade continued for 67 minutes — and the New Zealand cruiser fired the last shots at the Japanese mainland. *Achilles* sailed with most of the British Pacific Fleet for Australia on 11 August, but a small detachment — including *Gambia* — stayed back in Japanese waters to help the Americans cover carrier-borne attacks on industrial targets near Tokyo.

These spectacular actions did not reduce other New Zealand activities around the Pacific. During these months the RNZAF continued to operate against residual Japanese forces in New Britain, flying principally from Green Island. The squadrons moved to Jacquinot Bay in May, and the following month, the other units at Emirau were ordered to advance to Borneo, via Los

Negros. There were rumours of a role in Japan, but in the end no RNZAF squadrons moved beyond the operational areas to which they had been restricted by the United States.

'Tube Alloys' and the end of the war

Allied plans to bring the war to Japan itself were well advanced by early 1945, and from New Zealand's perspective the question was not whether the army should be deployed, but where and how. Any land contribution would have to be under the British, opening up prospects of joining the campaign in Burma. 2 NZ Divison was well equipped for the purpose, and the power it could develop in the field was evident in the final battles across northern Italy.[60] However, as late as September 1944, Churchill had to admit that they did not know precisely where to deploy the 'massive forces' that Britain was 'ardent to engage against the enemy'.[61] It was January 1945 before he invited Fraser to consider New Zealand's role.[62] There were two alternatives: joining South East Asia command under Mountbatten and fighting in Burma or Sumatra, or returning the division to New Zealand and re-forming later 'for operations in the Pacific ... either in conjunction with the Australian divisions or as a unit in a United States force'.[63] Churchill's own views were clear:

> *We should, of course, rejoice in the accession of your Division to the Commonwealth forces operating in South-East Asia Command. The development of operations for the conquest of the Japanese-occupied territories in this theatre depends both upon the quantity and the quality of the forces which we can build up against the enemy. The presence with us of the New Zealanders would thus bring at once a contribution of the first order.*[64]

The decision was complicated by New Zealand's manpower problems, which continued to frame decision-making in Wellington. On the basis of ground experience to that point in the islands, Allied planners could not see the war with Japan ending before late 1946, and pessimistic estimates suggested 1947 — all accompanied by very heavy casualties. In February 1945, Fraser told 2 NZ Division's commander, Lieutenant-General Sir Bernard Freyberg, that replacement drafts had been approved for April and June; but '...we have exhausted Grade A men except for 3,200 still held on appeal and ... some 3,500 who come of age each year'.[65] He continued:

> *While ... our immediate manpower problems may be surmounted it is difficult to see what can be done for remainder of period of hostilities, assuming JAPANESE WAR will NOT conclude for another two years ... Mr CHURCHILL suggests following broad alternatives for employment of SECOND DIVISION ... (a) To operate in South East Asia Command under Admiral Mountbatten (b) To return to NZ and thereafter possibly to be reformed for operations in Pacific under UNITED STATES COMMAND, either in conjunction with AUSTRALIAN DIVISIONS or as a unit in a UNITED STATES force...*[66]

In early April 1945, Cabinet decided that the most New Zealand could field during 1946 and 'possibly also 1947', in addition to the RNZN's ships and the RNZAF's 19 squadrons, was a 'land force 15,000 strong' of two brigades.[67] The idea met strong opposition in army circles; Puttick again raised the possibility of attaching a Fijian brigade, while Freyberg was 'strongly against [a] small division' and 'in favour of fighting Japanese with heavy equipment rather than infantry'.[68] Caucus leaned towards reorganising the force overseas rather than back in New Zealand — otherwise it would be 'nearer to 1947' before it could be made ready. But as Nash warned, the move would 'certainly cause disappointment to men and relatives alike'. He feared 'incidents'.[69] Fraser tried to consult Freyberg, but the latter was embroiled in final preparations for the Buckland operation in Italy and could not comment to any great extent.[70]

Victory in Europe clarified the situation, though Freyberg thought it would still not be possible to field a force in Asia or the Pacific before the end of 1945, warning Fraser that Burma and Singapore could 'be taken before New Zealand forces can be redeployed'.[71] He nonetheless canvassed his old friend and former commander, Lieutenant-General Sir Oliver Leese, on the uses of the existing four-brigade division in Leese's South East Asian command. 'You know personally how delighted I would be to have you and your division in this theatre,' Leese replied.[72] British opinion certainly leaned towards a South East Asian deployment,[73] though both the Chief of Imperial General Staff (CIGS) and Freyberg remained opposed to two-brigade divisions,[74] and the argument was batted back and forth during June.

At the beginning of July, Churchill told Fraser that Britain intended to provide five infantry divisions — possibly including the two proposed New Zealand brigades — to join US forces in 'the assault on Japan'.[75] Fraser could immediately promise only air and naval support; the army issue had become political and he felt that 'unless there is the largest degree of unanimity in parliament, a firm commitment cannot be entered into'.[76] It was early August before he was able to confirm that New Zealand could field two brigades with British forces for Operation Coronet, the invasion of Honshu due to be launched in March 1946.[77] The issue was not clear-cut. Freyberg reported from London that the New Zealand division would be an add-on to a British Commonwealth force, and 'General MacArthur will have to agree to this'. He liked the idea, however, because it 'enables us to get clear of jungle fighting and we will be used in our traditional role, together with all our guns and heavy equipment'.[78]

Allied projections in May 1945 suggested that although Japanese industrial strength was declining under the impact of US bombing and material shortages, the country could nonetheless deploy 96 divisions totalling 3,100,000 men to defend the homeland, Manchuria, Korea and northern China. A large percentage of these forces were in Japan itself, and the *Ketsu Go* (Decisive) scheme, adopted in March 1945, called for an increase in home defences to 60 divisions and 34 brigades — some 2.9 million men — backed by 10,000 aircraft, of which half were nominated for suicide missions.[79] These schemes were known to the Allies.[80] There was no easy way of defeating them, and MacArthur planned a two-phase assault. Operation Olympic was scheduled for the end of October,[81] and would have pushed three Army and one Marine Corps ashore in Kyushu — just over 550,000 men under General Walter Krueger — backed by 66 aircraft carriers and 2600 combat aircraft. They would have been up against just under 750,000 Japanese troops.

This huge operation was merely the prelude to Operation Coronet, the invasion of Honshu scheduled for March 1946. This would have thrown 28 divisions ashore, including the British Commonwealth force, supported by the entire US Navy and the British Pacific Fleet. They would have faced massive opposition, potentially including a civilian population armed with everything from guns to bludgeons. The attack would have been backed by an intense bombing campaign totalling 115,000 tons a month, delivered variously by B-29's based at Tinian; the 8th Air Force — due to shift from Europe to Okinawa — and the British Very Long Range bomber squadron, which included many New Zealand aircrew.

Allied logistics plans were predicated around the assumption that fighting would not end before November 1946,[82] and projections in April 1945 suggested that the invasion of Kyushu alone would incur more than half a million Allied casualties.[83] The whole campaign was thought likely to cost a million US casualties, 'and half that number of British'[84] — quite apart from a Japanese death toll likely to be in multiples of that figure, and continued suffering of the civilian population both in Japan and the bypassed zones of occupation in China and South East Asia, where Japanese military authority continued to hold sway.

This cost was not something the Allies took lightly; and as the extent of Japanese preparations unfolded to Allied intelligence sources in June, Nimitz quietly withdrew his backing from both attacks.[85] The question then was finding alternatives. Starving the Japanese out was one option: the Allies had complete control of the sea and a full blockade of the Home Islands in place. One scheme floated during 1945 called for chemical attacks on the Japanese rice crop, coupled with precision bombing to destroy the rail network. The latter was actually implemented; and the practical food situation in May 1946 highlights the effects that the full strategy would have had, when even with Allied food support, Japan's daily ration fell to 1046 calories. Without the rice crop and Allied support, there is little question that hundreds of thousands of Japanese would have died from starvation during the winter of 1945–46, along with many of the 300,000-odd Allied POWs and civilian internees in Japanese hands.[86]

All these options — military and general logistic — carried substantial human costs. However, there was a further option: the atomic bomb. Although also horrific, and in most respects more so than the other alternatives, rthis weapon carried the potential through its sheer violence to persuade the Japanese administration to agree to the Allied demand for unconditional surrender, and in a shorter time-frame than invasion. Although the only target could be civilians, there was also every potential for fewer total casualties, including among the Japanese whose population, Allied command believed, would also fight.

The option was made possible by the fact that, by mid-1945, the US project to develop an atomic bomb was nearing fruition. It was, again, a result of long-lead planning, something primarily driven by the European rather than the Pacific situation: the likely consequences of Nazi hegemony over Europe, opened up by the fall of France and subsequent war developments in 1940, demanded extreme measures. The project had actually been instituted by the United States, at British prompting, two months before Pearl Harbor. The task was neither easy nor quick, even with the vast resources of the United States and its allies behind it. Hundreds of physicists and technicians were involved, including several from New Zealand's DSIR, who joined physicists at Oak Ridge and Berkeley to fine-tune the calutrons that isolated fissionable material from the raw uranium.[87]

All of this took a significant amount of time: and as events panned out, these weapons were not needed to defeat the Nazis. However, by 1945 the designs for several potential types of atomic bomb were complete, production of the first bombs was under way, and although the performance of the various engineering approaches was still theoretical, the science behind them was sound. They were expected to work, and debate over whether to use the new weapons against Japan began raging in US command circles during April. The recommendation to do so was finally made, by committee, in June.[88] British confirmation came on 4 July. The motive, as Churchill later put it, was a 'merciful abridgement' of the war — an end in 'one or two violent shocks'.[89]

The first bomb was successfully tested while Allied leaders were meeting in Potsdam later that month. Armed with this stick, Truman and Churchill, backed by Chiang Kai-shek, produced the 'Three-Power' or 'Potsdam' declaration demanding unconditional surrender from Japan. New Zealand was not formally told until 7 August.[90] However, although the new government of Admiral Suzuki Kantaro had been seeking an end to the war, they would not surrender unconditionally. And so, on 6 August, a B-29 heavy bomber, *Enola Gay*, operating from Tinian, dropped a uranium-based bomb on Hiroshima.

Japanese physicists analysed the effects and were quickly able to tell their government the nature of what had been deployed against the civilians of Hiroshima. It was something entirely new in the history of warfare. However, a factional deadlock between hawks and doves prevented action by the Suzuki government for some days. The balance was tipped by the Soviet declaration of war on 8 August, followed by the use of a plutonium-based bomb on Nagasaki the following day and a US declaration that they would continue to use similar weapons. This was not entirely bluff; a third bomb was available and more were under construction. But they did not have to be deployed. Emperor Hirohito intervened, and despite significant ongoing opposition from some army circles, agreed to surrender. A cease-fire was declared on 15 August.

At the time nobody was quite sure how that would actually pan out, and New Zealand was caught amidst a final drama at sea. The signal to cease hostilities was flying at 11.23 am that day when a Japanese aircraft appeared over the fleet, apparently bent on attacking *Gambia*. American F4U Corsairs swarmed to shoot down the interloper. Parts of the aircraft fell on *Gambia's* quarterdeck, and the bomb exploded between the cruiser and the armoured fleet carrier *Indefatigable*. 'No further attacks were made,' the Naval Board subsequently reported 'but several "snoopers" were shot down by patrolling aircraft out of sight of the fleet, which retired to await events'.[91]

Three weeks later *Gambia* was one of 400 Allied ships, covered by 1200 aircraft, that entered Sagami Wan and the approaches to Tokyo Bay. 'Hands went to general quarters ready for any treacherous move on the part of the Japanese, and battle ensigns were flown,' the Naval Board reported 'but the entry was without incident.'[92] *Gambia*'s crew remained on alert after anchoring. 'Watch remained at defence stations. Steam for slow speed.'[93] Motorboat patrols around the cruiser began just after 6.00 pm. The crew briefly went to air defence stations at dusk, and there was another precautionary alert at 4.00 am, in case of dawn attack. However, Japan seemed remarkably quiescent.

Gambia left for Tokyo Bay, to represent New Zealand at the surrender ceremonies, on 31 August, navigated through the Urago Straits by a Japanese pilot, a 'poor wizened up guy' who came aboard on the quarterdeck and had to 'walk right the length of the ship and up to the bridge. Well you can imagine, all the Matelots are looking at him … the enemy until a few days previously…'[94] The instrument of surrender was signed for New Zealand by Air Vice-Marshal Leonard M. Isitt, during a short ceremony on board the battleship USS *Missouri* on 2 September. Isitt was accompanied by Lieutenant J.D. Allingham of *Gambia*, and the cruiser's band was lent to the British flagship *Duke of York* for a sunset ceremony attended by Admiral Halsey — the first time the White Ensign had been hauled down since war had broken out, nearly six years earlier.

The 'whole task', as Churchill put it, was done.[95]

EPILOGUE

The Legacy of War

Plans by the New Zealand government to send a division to Japan evaporated in wake of the Japanese surrender. The New Zealand government needed only a contingent for the Commonwealth Occupation Force, and the men of 9 Brigade — part of 2 NZ Division, then still in Italy — were given the task. Renamed Jayforce, the brigade prepared for its task in Italy, under Brigadier K.L. Stewart, and left for Kure in February the following year.

Virtually everyone else came home, though it was still 1946 before the last servicemen returned. New Zealand prisoners at Singapore were an early priority, and Squadron Leader M.L. Pirie had Dakotas fitted out as air ambulances soon after the Japanese surrender. However, he could not despatch them until Singapore was formally reclaimed by the British on 2 September. The first Dakotas landed at Kallang 11 days later and brought back 156 New Zealanders. They were too late for some, including Evan Baxter and John Haberfield, New Zealanders with the Fleet Air Arm who had been captured during the Palembang raid. They were executed at Changi, officially a fortnight before the Japanese surrender — but by some accounts a week later, before Allied forces could relieve the occupied areas.[1]

The Pacific war had been a remarkable national experience for New Zealand. For the first time in its history, the country came under direct threat — certainly of strangulation, potentially of invasion. The immediate tactical lessons were clear. As a maritime nation more than 1000 miles (1600 km) from the nearest land-mass, New Zealand relied absolutely on air and sea power for survival. The lack of fighter aircraft in 1942 — notably to protect essential defences along the vulnerable communications routes, well away from New

Zealand's own shores — compounded the crisis that year. The same experience had proven that, when the crunch came, New Zealand could not rely on pre-war arrangements to get the necessary aircraft. After the war, successive governments ensured that New Zealand was never again without its own fighter protection.[2] It was 60 years before the policy was changed.

New Zealand participated as fully as it could in the Pacific war, partly for pragmatic reasons but also because the Fraser administration, quite explicitly, wanted to 'ensure that when the future of the Pacific is being considered after the war we ... are in the most favourable possible political position'.[3] This must be understood in proper context. History can seldom be reduced to neat images, and the policy was not simply a function of an emerging independence from Britain. It was evident to the New Zealand government, even before the fall of Singapore, that the collective security systems of the inter-war period had failed. Fraser's efforts to persuade Britain to restore protection, evidenced by his pleading calls for Hudson bombers and fighter aircraft, also failed. In 1940–42 New Zealand therefore turned to America for succour — but this matched Britain's similar moves, and the shift was couched within the framework of Commonwealth. This was the initial context under which Fraser pushed an active New Zealand contribution, as he remarked to Churchill in 1942, 'to the fullest extent of our capacity'.[4] The main motive was his desire to improve New Zealand's apparent lack of weight in British command circles, not to gain independent credibility post-war with the United States or, initially, to exert New Zealand's voice on the world stage.[5]

How then does this relate to the relationship with the United States and the emergence of what F.L.W. Wood called a 'small power rampant'[6] — New Zealand as an independent world voice? Wood's observation, which is not without foundation, contradicts the equally well-founded point that New Zealand, in Churchill's words, was 'with' Britain 'from the moment when ... war was loosed upon the world'.[7] The paradox has attracted extensive analysis,[8] but it seems clear that although nascent in the early war years, the real impetus for New Zealand's international 'rampancy' did not come until 1943–44, when both Australia and New Zealand were sidelined in any post-war Pacific settlements. Despite contributing forces from all three services, producing virtually all the food for the Pacific war effort, and providing base facilities for US troops, New Zealand was excluded from the 1943 Cairo agreement on post-war Pacific affairs. So was Australia, and there was a direct link between the Pacific carve-up foreshadowed in the Cairo Declaration and the Australian-initiated Canberra Pact. That led directly to the exclusion of New Zealand from the military side of the New Britain campaign — in other words, to restrictions on any future ability to swap 'contribution for status'.

The result was a new approach: a more vigorous regional policy and an assertion of national independence. However, from Fraser's point of view this was still overlaid across a Commonwealth structure; to him, the Commonwealth was an 'association of independent democratic nations',[9] and within that structure New Zealand had — as he put it — 'independence with something added'.[10] Certainly his own policies, which he pursued until the Labour government was defeated in the 1949 elections, matched this view.[11]

However, the effort to buy a 'favourable political position' did not count for much in the longer term. Japan, reformed and rebuilt under MacArthur's effective dictatorship, was quickly viewed as a buffer against the Soviets. At the 1948 Commonwealth Conference, only Australia and New Zealand voiced concern about a further possible Japanese threat.[12] By 1950, when the Korean war broke out, Japan was widely viewed as a friend to the west. Australasian efforts to establish the ANZUS pact, initially and overtly as a buffer against a potentially resurgent Japan, were fraught with difficulty.

These political issues ran alongside the deep social impact of the war. As a whole, the Second World War had a decisive effect, but it seems clear that in some respects the Pacific aspect of the near six-year struggle had a greater direct impact on New Zealand's general populace than the European. Although New Zealand joined Britain in the war against Germany in 1939 – and faced local threats to its shipping from German auxiliary cruisers — it was only in late 1941 when the war spread fully to the Pacific that the struggle really arrived on New Zealand's doorstep. Total mobilisation, the threat of starvation or invasion, renewed shortages, blackouts and the arrival of US troops in 1942 all contributed to a significant level of social and cultural pressure.

These developments, shared by the wider population, extended and intensified the exigencies of the inter-war depression era. The generation that emerged from the war in the late 1940s knew only economic hardship. Many had spent their formative years in families broken by wartime separation or loss, and many had lived through the uncertain months of 1942 when — at popular level at least — many loved ones were fighting in Europe, and the Japanese did not seem far away.

This experience unquestionably shaped a generational world-view, contributing in no small measure to the conscious effort by successive New Zealand governments during and after the Second World War to create a prosperous, safe, stable and family-oriented society in the 1950s and beyond.

To a large part they succeeded; and the fact that this society was not wanted in the longer term, as new generations grew to adulthood, does not alter the intent of the day. Despite ongoing sentiment for Britain, the war and its legacy also reinforced a parallel and emerging sense of nationhood, driving overt policies to build New Zealand as a viable and self-sufficient nation; to complete national road, rail, power and energy projects, and to protect New Zealand economically, politically and physically from the outside world. Foreign domination, either directly by occupation or indirectly through foreign control of national industry, finances and state-owned infrastructure, was unthinkable. New Zealand had stared that threat down in 1942.

Collective defence was another key priority. New Zealand's search for security through ANZUS, direct ties with Australia and with the FPDA, along with the provision of a wide range of capabilities for New Zealand's own forces — albeit on a small scale — reflected the experience of 1942 when collective imperial security failed. These issues were deep-seated and enduring. When a new generation came to power in the mid-1980s that rejected the thinking of the wartime generation, their response was merely to reverse many of the principles in order to undo what had been rejected, but without transcending the basic frameworks. This included imposing a programme of state asset sales from the late 1980s which, curiously, closely matched the mechanisms by which the Japanese, had they conquered New Zealand, intended to exploit the local economy to their own benefit.

All this took a further generation to work through, and it was the early twenty-first century before a generation emerged that had not been obviously affected — either by participation or in some aspect of its experience, upbringing or thinking — by the total war of 1939-45 and its aftermath.

Notes

Chapter 1: The Road to War
1. *In Time of War — Selections from the Wartime Addresses of the Rt. Hon. Peter Fraser*, Government Print, Wellington 1946, p. 17.
2. *NZ Herald*, 16 March 1942.
3. See, e.g. M.C. Fairbrother, (ed) Documents Relating to New Zealand's Participation in the Second World War, Vol. III, War History Branch, Department of Internal Affairs, Wellington, 1963, New Zealand Liaison Officer (London) to the Chief of the General Staff (Wellington), 27 March 1942, pp. 251-54. Hereafter cited as *Documents*, Vol. III.
4. Winston Churchill, *The Second World War*, Vol. III, Cassell & Co, London 1950, p. 515.
5. Ibid, p. 516.
6. Nicholas Tarling, *A Sudden Rampage — The Japanese occupation of Southeast Asia, 1941-45*, Hurst & Co., London 2001.p. 11.
7. G. W. Monger, *The End of Isolation*, Thomas Nelson & Sons, London 1963, pp. 10-11.
8. See, e.g. P. A. Towle, 'The Effect of the Russo-Japanese War on British Naval Policy', *Mariner's Mirror* Vol 60, No.4, November 1970.
9. G. Grenwood & C. Grimshad (eds), *Documents on Australian International Affairs, 1901-1918* (D.A.) (Thomas Nelson (Australia) Ltd, Melbourne 1977) pp 143-45.
10. *NZ Herald*, July 3 1905, p 4.
11. *New Zealand Parliamentary Debates* (NZPD) Vol 143 1908, pp 554-89.
12. *Evening Post*, editorial 12 August 1908.
13. Matthew Wright, *Blue Water Kiwis*, Reed NZ Ltd, Auckland 2001, pp. 19-28.
14. Ibid, p. 63.
15. AJHR 1922 A-5 'Conference of the limitation of armaments', pp 12-13.
16. Richard Storry, *A History of Modern Japan*, Penguin, London 1960, p. 163
17. Ian Sturton (ed), *Conway's All the World's Battleships*, Conway Maritime Press, London 1987, pp. 93-99, 129-131, 178-183.
18. AJHR 1927 A-7 'Singapore and Naval Defence' p. 2. See also Wright, *Blue Water Kiwis*, pp. 68-69.
19. John B. Hattendorf 'American Strategies in the Pacific War', in Crawford, John (ed), *Kia Kaha, New Zealand in the Second World War*, Oxford University Press, Melbourne, 2002, reprint. pp. 37-38.
20. Storry, p. 172.
21. Wright, *Blue Water Kiwis*, p. 76.
22. Storry, pp. 200-201
23. Tarling, p. 43.
24. Sturton (ed), p. 129.
25. NZPD Vol 246 p 539.
26. NA PM 86/27/10, Verbatim Report of Proceedings, speech by C. A. Berendsen to the Defence Conference, 1939.
27. Winston Churchill, *The Second World War*, Vol. III, pp. 518-519. Heinz Magenheimer, *Hitler's War*, esp. pp. 53-58, argues that both Hitler and Stalin viewed this pact as expedient.
28. Matthew Wright, *Kiwi Air Power*, Reed, Auckland 1998, pp. 22-25.

29 Ibid, p. 30.
30 Ibid, p. 34.
31 *Documents*, Vol. III, pp. 267-273.
32 Hattendorf p. 40. See also Exhibits of the Joint Committee, PHA Pt. 15 pp 1485-1550, 'United States-British Staff Conversation'; Hearings before the Joint Committee on the Investigation of the Pearl Harbor Attack, Part 33, Exhibit No. 4, 'Rainbow-5'; Senator David I. Walsh 'The Decline and the Renaissance of the Navy 1922-1944', US Government Printing Office, Washington, 1944.
33 *Documents*, Vol. III, Governor-General of New Zealand to the SSDA, 15 June 1950, pp. 206-07.
34 F. L. W. Wood, *Political and External Affairs*, War Histories Branch, Wellington 1958, p. 198.
35 Tarling, p. 53; Barber p. 81.
36 *Documents*, Vol. III, Secretary of State for Dominion Affairs (SSDA) to the Governor-General of New Zealand, 2 July 1940, p. 3.
37 Op cit, SSDA to the HIgh Commissioner for the United Kingdom (Wellington)., 14 July 1940, p. 1
38 Op cit, Governor-General of New Zealand to the SSDA, 30 July 1940, p. 14.
39 Op cit, Governor-General of New Zealand to the SSDA, 5 August 1940, pp. 207-08.
40 Op cit, SSDA to the High Commissioner for the United Kingdom (Wellington), 11 August 1940, pp. 18-19.
41 Churchill, *The Second World War*, Vol. III, pp 157-58
42 See, e.g. Michael Ashby, 'Fraser's Foreign Policy', in Margaret Clark (ed), *Peter Fraser, Master Politician*, Dunmore Press, Palmerston North, 1998, p., 169.
43 Tarling, p. 59.
44 *Documents*, Vol. III, SSDA to the Governor-General of New Zealand, 26 June 1940, p. 6.
45 Churchill, *The Second World War*, Vol. III, p. 159.
46 Ibid, p. 156.
47 Barber, p. 82.
48 *Documents*, Vol. III, SSDA to the Acting Prime Minister of New Zealand, 22 July 1941, p. 45.
49 Op cit, Walter Nash to Peter Fraser, 24 July 1941, p. 46.
50 Wright, *Kiwi Air Power*, pp. 64-68.
51 S. W. Roskill, *The War At Sea*, Vol I., HM Stationery Office, London pp 555-56.
52 Churchill, *The Second World War*, Vol. III, p. 525.
53 Ibid, p. 527, 534.
54 *Documents*, Vol. III, SSDA to the Prime Minister of New Zealand, 4 December 1941, pp. 88-89.
55 Op cit, SSDA to the Prime Minister of New Zealand, 5 December 1941, pp. 90-91
56 Op cit, SSDA to the Prime Minister of New Zealand, 7 December 1941, p. 98.
57 Waters, p. 250, n. 2. See also Laurie Barber and Ken Henshall, *The Last War of Empires — Japan and the Pacific War, 1941-45*, David Bateman, Auckland 1999. p. 98, n.2.
58 There were exceptions, for instance Lieutenant-General Sir Bernard Freyberg. Matthew Wright, *Desert Duel*, Reed NZ Ltd, Auckland 2002, pp. 169-170.
59 Roskill, I., p. 560.
60 *Documents*, Vol. III, Governor-Genral of New Zealand to the SSDA, 13 June 1940, p. 206.
61 *NZ Herald*, 15 December 1941.
62 Roskill, I, p. 566.
63 W. H. Garzke & R. O. Dulin, *British, Soviet, French and Dutch Battleships of World War II*, Jane's, London 1980, pp 192-208, 244-45.
64 Harrison. p. 91.
65 Paul Harrison, Brian Lockstone and Andy Anderson, *The Golden Age of New Zealand Flying Boats*, Random House, Auckland 1997, p 91
66 *NZ Herald*, 11 December 1941.
67 *The Press*, 5 January 1942.
68 *Documents*, Vol. III, No. 113, Prime Minister of New Zealand to the SSDA, 30 December 1941, pp 114-15.
69 Archibald Wavell, 'The Operations in the South West Pacific, 15th January 1942 to 25th

70 February 1942', HMSO, London 1948, p. 2.
70 Ibid, p. 3.
71 Ibid, p. 4.
72 Ibid, p. 7.
73 Cited in Dr Cathy Downes 'A Kiwi Naval Officer at Singapore, 1941' in *Navy Today* No. 65, April 2002.
74 Barber, p. 105.
75 Norman Dixon, *On the Psychology of Military Incompetence*, Pimlico, London, 1976, pp. 130-144.
76 NA AIR 102/5/1 Misc. Malayan Campaign notes by RNZAF officers, memo by P L Laing, 1 April 1942.
77 Described by R Tyers, memoir in McCarthy p 32.
78 Churchill, *The Second World War*, Vol. IV, Cassell & Co., London 1951, p. 83.
79 Ibid, p. 83.
80 Ibid, p. 85.
81 F. A. McCarthy 'Running the Gauntlet out from Singapore', *Contact*, Vol 1 No. 12, March 1942.
82 NA AIR 102/5/1 Misc. Malayan Campaign notes by RNZAF officers, Report from OC C & A Flight to CO No.1 NZ ACU, 13 February 1942.
83 Described by M. T. B. Harris, memoir in McCarthy p 38
84 Wavell, p. 13.
85 RNZN Museum Oral History DLA 0073 Able Seaman L. C. Hurndell
86 Ibid.
87 Churchill, The Second World War, Vol. IV, p. 89.
88 Wavell, p. 11.
89 Bill Gunston, *Japanese and Italian Aircraft*, Salamander, London 1985, pp. 49-53
90 Barber, pp. 107-108.
91 Ibid, p. 113.
92 Wavell, p.15.
93 Downes, p. 11.
94 Barber p. 115; Carl Bridge, 'Australia, New Zealand and Allied grand strategy, 1941-43', in John Crawford (ed), *Kia Kaha*, Oxford, Melbourne 2002, p. 60.

Chapter 2: Desperate Defence
1 *Documents*, Vol. III, The Prime Minister of New Zealand to the SSDA, 19 February 1942, p. 229.
2 Cited in Wright. *Kiwi Air Power*, p. 22.
3 *Documents*, Vol. III, New Zealand Liaison Officer (London) to the Chief of the General Staff (Wellington), 27 March 1942, pp. 251-254.
4 *NZ Herald*, 9 December 1941.
5 Ibid.
6 Ibid, 15 December 1941.
7 Ibid, 16 December 1941.
8 Waters, p. 212.
9 NA Navy Department Series 1 Operations HMNZS *Monowai* Encounter with submarine and aircraft, January 1942. 'Report of action between HMNZS *Monowai* and U-boat.'
10 RNZN Oral History, Lieutenant-Commander S W Hicks, RNZN (Rtd).
11 Ibid.
12 NA Navy Department Series 1 Operations HMNZS Monowai Encounter with submarine and aircraft, January 1942. 'Report of action between HMNZS Monowai and U-boat.'
13 *Southern Cross*, 26 July 1949.
14 *Evening Post*, 27 July 1942.
15 Waters, p. 219.
16 *Documents*, Vol. III, No. No. 209, Prime Minister to the New Zealand Minister, Washington, 13 March 1942, p. 236.
17 Op cit, Chief of the General Staff (Wellington) to the New Zealand Liaison Officer (London), 27 February 1942, pp. 231-232.

18 Op cit, Prime Minister of New Zealand to the Prime Minister of the United Kingdom, 28 February 1942.
19 Ibid, p. 22.
20 *NZ Herald*, 16 March 1942.
21 Matthew Wright, *Desert Duel*, Reed, Auckland 2002, p. xx.
22 *NZ Herald*, 9 March 1942.
23 *NZ Herald*, 11 March 1942.
24 Ibid.
25 *NZ Herald*, 10 March 1942.
26 Ross, pp. 32-33.
27 Paul Harrison, et al, *The Golden Age of New Zealand Flying Boats*, p. 97.
28 Wright, *Kiwi Air Power*, pp. 31, 46.
29 See Matthew Wright, *Blue Water Kiwis*, Reed, Auckland 2001, pp. 91-98.
30 Harrison et al, p. 75.
31 Ibid, pp. 94-99
32 *Documents*, Vol. III, No. 191 Governor-General of New Zealand to the SSDA, 4 December 1940.
33 Waters, pp. 2230224.
34 *Documents*, Vol. III, No. 193, Acting Prime Minister of New Zealand to the SSDA, 4 September 1941.
35 Nancy M. Taylor, *The Home Front*, Internal Affairs, Wellington 1986, pp. 480-573
36 Matthew Wright, *Quake - Hawke's Bay 1931*, Reed, Auckland 2002.
37 Matthew Wright, *Town and Country*, HDC, Hastings 2001, p. 524
38 J. Wright, pers. comm.
39 *NZ Herald*, 6 March 1942.
40 *NZ Herald*, 9 March 1942.
41 Ibid.
42 *Documents*, Vol. III, Fraser to Nash, 13 March 1942, Section IV, p. 241
43 Op cit, Chief of the General Staff to General Freyberg, GOC 2nd NZEF (Egypt), 2 January 1942, pp.217-218.
44 *Auckland Star*, 11 March 1942.
45 Ibid.
46 *Documents*, Vol. III, Prime Minister of New Zealand to the SSDA, 19 February 1942, p. 228.
47 Op cit, Prime Minister of New Zealand to the SSDA, 30 January 1942, p. 218.
48 Op cit, SSDA to the Prime Minister of New Zealand, 3 February 1942, p. 219-220.
49 Op cit, Prime Minister of New Zealand to the SSDA, 4 February 1942, pp. 220-21
50 Op cit, SSDA to the Prime Minister of New Zealand, 3 February 1942, p. 222-23.
51 Op cit, New Zealand Liaison Officer (London) to the Chief of the General Staff (Wellington), 27 March 1942, pp. 251-254
52 NA EA 1 PM 85/1/22 General 'Japanese Plans for the Invasion of New Zealand', Unclassified Intelligence Report, E.H.F. Svensson, attachment.
53 Op cit, Memorandum for Mr Wilson, 7-4-49.
54 Ibid.
55 NA EA 1 PM 85/1/22 General 'Japanese Plans for the Invasion of New Zealand', Unclassified Intelligence Report, E.H.F. Svensson, attachment.
56 NA EA 1 PM 85/1/22 General 'Japanese Plans for the Invasion of New Zealand', Unclassified Intelligence Report, E.H.F. Svensson, attachment.
57 Andrew Kershaw (ed), *Battle of the Pacific*, Phoebus, London 1975, p. 20.
58 Theodore F. Cook, Jr, 'Our Midway Disaster' in Robert Cowley (ed), *What If? - Military Historians imagine what might have been*, Pan, London 2001.
59 Ibid, p. 330.
60 *Documents*, Vol. III, No. 203, SSDA to the Prime Minister of New Zealand, 4 March 1942.
61 For an alternative see Carl Bridge, 'Australia, New Zealand and Allied grand strategy, 1941-43', in John Crawford (ed), *Kia Kaha*, Oxford, Melbourne 2002, p. 53.

62 Bridge, p. 53, argues at Churchill's suggestion.
63 Matthew Wright, *Desert Duel*, Reed, Auckland 2002, p. 32..
64 Warren F. Kimball (ed) Churchill & Roosevelt, The Complete Correspondence, Vol. I, p. 321.
65 *Documents*, Vol. III, High Commissioner for New Zealand (London) to the Prime Minister, 12 March 1942, p. 171; ibid, Prime Minister of Australia to the Secretary pf State for Dominion Affairs, 20 March 1942, pp. 176-77.
66 *Documents*, Vol. III, New Zealand Minister, Washington, to the Prime Minister of New Zealand, p. 149.
67 Churchill, *The Second World War*, Vol. III, p. 9.
68 Cited in Bridge, pp. 54-55.
69 *NZ Herald*, editorial, 16 March 1942.
70 Churchill, *The Second World War*, Vol. III, p. 15.
71 Kimball, 'To the Former Naval Person', p. 398.
72 Ibid, Roosevelt to Former Naval Person, 30 January 1942, p. 336-37.
73 *Documents*, Vol. III, SSDA to the Prime Minister of New Zealand, 23 March 1942, enclosures, p.180.
74 Op cit, New Zealand Minister, Washington, to the Prime Minister, 24 March 1942, p. 249.
75 Op cit, SSDA to the Prime Minister of New Zealand, 10 March 1942.
76 Op cit, New Zealand Minister, Washington, to the Prime Minister, 24 March 1942, p. 185.
77 Op cit, Prime Minister to the New Zealand Minister, Washington, 13 March 1942, pp. 236-237.
78 Waters pp. 259-260.
79 *Documents*, Vol. III, Prime Minister of New Zealand to the New Zealand Minister, Washington, 5 April 1942, pp. 201-202.
80 Op cit, Prime Minister of New Zealand to the New Zealand Minister, Washington, 19 March 1942, pp. 248-49.
81 Op cit, New Zealand Minister, Washington, to the Prime Minister, 27 March 1943.
82 Op cit, New Zealand Liaison Officer (London) to the Chief of the General Staff (Wellington), 27 March 1942, pp. 251-254.
83 Waters, pp. 261-263.
84 Ibid, p. 266; R. J. McDougall, *New Zealand Naval Vessels*, GP Books, Wellington 1989, pp. 64-74
85 See e.g. Kershaw (ed) pp. 20-27; Geoffrey Bennett, *Naval Battles of World War II*, David McKay, New York, 1975, pp. 169-175; Roskill,Vol II, p. 36.
86 Barber, p. 119, cites 233 American aircraft faced 261 Japanese.
87 Bennett, pp. 175-181; Kershaw (ed), pp. 28-37; Barber, pp. 120-121; Roskill, Vol II., pp. 36-42.
88 Edward Jablonski, *A Pictorial History of the World War II Years*, Wings Books, New York 1977, p. 296.

Chapter Three: Into the Islands
1 *Documents*, Vol. III, Memorandum from Lieutenant-General Puttick to the Minister of Defence, 3 August 1942, p. 359
2 S. L. Mayer (ed), *The Rise and Fall of Imperial Japan*, Bison, London 1976, p. 174.
3 Barber, p. 121; S. W. Roskill *The War At Sea* 1939-1945, Vol II, HM Stationery Office, London 1956, p. 42.
4 Roskill, Vol. II, p. 33.
5 Cited in Gillespie p. 107.
6 *Documents*, Vol. III, Prime Minister of New Zealand to the New Zealand Minister, Washington, 27 June 1942, p. 265
7 Op cit, Prime Minister of New Zealand to the New Zealand Minister, Washington, 19 June 1942, p. 262.
8 Op cit, Prime Minister of New Zealand to the New Zealand Minister, Washington, 27 June 1942, p. 264.
9 Ibid, p. 265.
10 Op cit, Prime Minister of New Zealand to the New Zealand Minister, Washington, 27 June 1942, p. 265.

11 Op cit, Prime Minister of New Zealand to the New Zealand Minister, Washington, 19 June 1942, p. 262-63.
12 Op cit, Prime Minister of New Zealand to the New Zealand Minister, Washington, 27 June 1942, p. 266
13 Ross, pp. 128-129.
14 *Documents*, Vol. III, New Zealand Legation (Washington) to the Prime Minister of New Zealand, 8 July 1942, p. 349.
15 Op cit, Chief of the General Staff (Wellington) to the New Zealand Liaison Officer (London), p. 350.
16 Op cit, Memorandum from Lieutenant-General Puttick to the Minister of Defence, 31 July 1942, p. 351.
17 Ibid, pp. 352-353; see also Gillespie, p. 47.
18 *Documents*, Vol. III, Memorandum from Lieutenant-General Puttick to the Minister of Defence, 3 August 1942, pp. 358-359
19 Ibid.
20 Op cit, New Zealand Legation (Washington) to the Prime Minister of New Zealand, 8 July 1942, p. 349.
21 Kershaw (ed), p. 41.
22 Roskill, Vol II., p. 222.
23 Ibid, pp. 225-26
24 Bennett, pp. 194-195, Kershaw (ed), pp. 41-43.
25 William H. Garzke and Robert O. Dulin, *Battleships: United States Battleships in World War II*, MacDonald and Janes, London 1976, pp. 38-39.
26 Waters, pp. 298-299.
27 Ibid, p. 46-47.
28 Kershaw (ed), p. 48.
29 *Documents*, Vol. III, Memorandum from Lieutenant-General Puttick to the Minister of Defence, 3 September 1942.
30 Op cit, Memorandum from Lieutenant-General Puttick to the Minister of Defence, 16 October 1942.
31 Op cit, Memorandum from Lieutenant-General Puttick to the Minister of Defence, 20 October 1942.
32 Op cit, Memorandum from Lieutenant-General Puttick to the Minister of Defence, 2 November 1942.
33 — *Pacific Kiwis*, Reed, Wellington, n.d., p. 36.
34 Gillespie p. 86.
35 *Documents*, Vol. III, Letter from Major-General Barrowclough to Lieutenant-General Puttick, 17 January 1943, p. 368.
36 Ibid, p. 370.
37 *Documents*, Vol. III, Memorandum from the Deputy Chief of the General Staff to the Minister of Defence, 27 January 1943, p. 373.
38 Op cit, War Cabinet Minute, 4 February 1943, pp. 374-75.
39 WTu MS-Papers 2001-008-054 Thompson, Eric Hardisty, 1922-2000: Papers, Charlie Nicholson's Green Island Story
40 *Documents*, Vol. III, Rt. Hon. J. G. Coates (Noumea) to the Prime Minister, 24 February 1943, p. 375.
41 Gillespie, pp. 104-105.
42 *Documents*, Vol. III, p. 375, n. 2.
43 Op cit, Lieutenant-General Puttick to Major-General Barrowclough, 18 May 1943, p. 377. Puttick's italics.
44 Ibid.
45 Op cit, Prime Minister to Admiral Halsey, 30 August 1943, p. 405.
46 Matthew Wright, *Italian Odyssey*, Reed NZ Ltd, Auckland 2003, p. xx.
47 *Documents*, Vol. III, lMajor-General Barrowclough to Lieutenant-General Puttick, 24 May 1943, p. 380.

48 Op cit, Major-General Barrowclough to Lieutenant-General Puttick, 28 May 1943, p. 383.
49 Op cit, Major-General Barrowclough to Lieutenant-General Puttick, 30 May 1943, p. 383.
50 Op cit, Lieutenant-General Puttick to Admiral Halsey, 16 June 1943, pp. 386-87.
51 Op cit, Major-General Barrowclough to Lieutenant-General Puttick, 24 June 1943, p. 388.
52 Op cit, Lieutenant-General Puttick to Admiral Halsey, 19 June 1943, p., 388.
53 Op cit, Admiral Halsey to the Prime Minister, 21 August 1943, p. 404.
54 Op cit, Major-General Barrowclough to Lieutenant-General Puttick, 24 June 1943, p. 389.
55 Op cit, War Cabinet Minute 27 June 1943, pp 390-91.
56 Op cit, Colonel C. W. Salmon, New Zealand Chiefs of Staff Representative, to Admiral Halsey, 20 August 1943.
57 Op cit, Prime Minister to the Hon W. Perry, 2 August 1943, p. 402.
58 Gillespie, Appendix V, p. 341.
59 *Documents*, Vol. III, Colonel C. W. Salmon, New Zealand Chiefs of Staff Representative, to Admiral Halsey, 20 August 1943
60 Op cit, Admiral Halsey to the Prime Minister, 21 August 1943, p. 404.
61 Op cit, Prime Minister to Admiral Halsey, 30 August 1943, p. 405.
62 D.M. Skinner Collection, H. Skinner, hand-written note on 'New Zealand Free Lance' clipping, September 1, 1943.
63 Gillespie, pp. 114-115.
64 D. M. Skinner Collection, H. Skinner, letter home 7 September 1943
65 Op cit, H. Skinner, letter home 2 October 1943
66 WTu MS Papers 3907 Waterman Family Collection, letter to 'Dear Dad & All', 11 April 1943.
67 D. M. Skinner Collection, H. Skinner, letter home 20 August 1943.
68 Op cit, H. Skinner, letter home 2 September 1943.
69 Op cit, H. Skinner, letter home 21 September 1943
70 Op cit, H. Skinner, letter home 25 September 1943
71 WTu MS Papers 3907 Waterman Family Collection, letter to 'Dear Dad & All', 26 June 1943
72 Op cit, 11 April 1943.
73 —*Pacific Kiwis*, p. 47.
74 Ibid p. 42.
75 D. M. Skinner Collection, Ted Skinner, letter home 27 March 1943.
76 —*Pacific Saga*, p. 45.
77 D. M. Skinner Collection, Ted Skinner, letter home 27 March 1943.
78 Op cit, letter home 3 April 1943.
79 Ross, p. 130.
80 NA AIR 118/52 War History Narrative of life in Santo, Base Report, Appendix B-1 RNZAF Station Espiritu Santo. Extract from minutes of conference 5 September 1942.
81 NA AIR 131/24/3 DCAS to AMS, Minute 17 Oct 1942
82 NA AIR 118/52 War History Narrative of life in Santo, Base Report, Appendix B-1 RNZAF Station Espiritu Santo.
83 Ibid, 26 September 1942
84 NA AIR 118/52 War History Narrative of life in Santo, Base Report, Appendix B-1 RNZAF Station Espiritu Santo.
85 Op. cit., Interview with W/O M Harris 18-5-48.
86 WTu MS 0842, Morgan Papers, J Morgan diary, 13 October 1942.
87 *Ibid*, 27-28 October 1942.
88 Andrews, letter to Willy, c12 December 1942.
89 Gillespie, p. 292.
90 NA AIR 150/12 Personal Narrative of Experiences with 15 Squadron 1942-43, Basil A Berry
91 Op cit, Diary and Narrative of J J Mackie, 15 Squadron in Tonga and Santo, 18 Squadron in Solomons.
92 Ibid.
93 Ibid.
94 NA AIR 150/12 Personal Narrative of Experiences with 15 Squadron 1942-43, Basil A Berry
95 Ibid

96	Ibid.
97	WTu MS-Papers-7417-3, Andrew family: Papers, Richard Andrew, letters to his family and other papers; letter 'To Dearest Fred and Ef', 12 December 1943.
98	*Ibid*, 25 December 1942.
99	Waters, p. 033.
100	RNZN Navy Museum Oral History, J. L. W. Salter
101	Ibid.
102	NA Navy Department Series 1 16/8/40 Operations - HMNZS *Achilles*, encounter with Japanese dive-bomber, January 1943. CO HMNZS *Achilles* to Naval Secretary 17 May 1943.
103	Op cit, Acting CO HMNZS *Achilles* to Naval Secretary, Report on Damage, 5 January 1943.
104	RNZN Museum Oral History Sergeant P. H. Stapleton RM (Rtd). The description of the Oerlikon varies from Waters p. 306.
105	NA Navy Department Series 1 16/8/40 Operations - HMNZS *Achilles*, encounter with Japanese dive-bomber, January 1943. CO HMNZS *Achilles* to Naval Secretary 17 May 1943.
106	Op cit, CO HMNZS *Achilles* to Naval Secretary 17 May 1943, Appendix 2.
107	NA Navy Department Series 1 16/8/40 Operations - HMNZS *Achilles*, encounter with Japanese dive-bomber, January 1943. CO HMNZS *Achilles* to Naval Secretary 17 May 1943
108	RNZN Museum Oral History Warrant Mechanician R. W. Kirkwood RNZN (Rtd)
109	RNZN Museum Oral History DLB0004 Yeoman of Signals J. L. W. Salter BEM, MID, RNZNVR (Rtd).
11	Waters, p. 309.
111	Mayer (ed), p. 169.
112	NA Navy Department Series 1 6/36/2 Ships and Repairs, HMNZ Ships — loss of or damage to. 'Loss of HMNZS *Moa* due to enemy action.' 'Report on Loss of *Moa* 12 March [sic] 1943'.
113	Ibid.
114	Ibid.
115	Op cit, Report on Loss of *Moa* 12 March [sic] 1943'
116	Barber, p. 138.
117	NA Navy Department Series 1 16/8/43, Operations... HMNZS *Leander* - Encounter with Japanese Naval Forces, Kula Gulf, July 1943. CO HMNZS *Leander* to Naval Secretary, Navy Office: 'Report of action against Japanese naval forces', 13 July 1943.
118	Ibid.
119	Not seven as noted in Waters p. 321. *Op cit*, Navy Office to Registrar Births Deaths and Marriages 25 September 1944. The men were: Able Seaman James F. Beattie, Able Seaman George G. Dryland, Stoker 1st Class G. C. Edwards, Able Seaman Frank W. Hooke, Able Seaman Robert G. Morris, Stoker 1st Class Maurice W. O'Neill, Acting Leading Seaman Raymond A. Rolston, all of the RNZN, and Royal Navy Able Seaman William D. Clyde.
120	Ibid.
121	CO HMNZS *Leander* to Naval Secretary, Navy Office: 'Report of action against Japanese naval forces', 13 July 1943
122	Ibid.
123	RNZN Museum Oral History Chief Electrician R. B. Harvey B.E.M., RNZN (Rtd).
124	CO HMNZS *Leander* to Naval Secretary, Navy Office: 'Report of action against Japanese naval forces', 13 July 1943
125	RNZN Museum Oral History DLA 0013 Commander G. Mitchell MBE, RNZN (Rtd).
126	CO HMNZS *Leander* to Naval Secretary, Navy Office: 'Report of action against Japanese naval forces', 13 July 1943
127	Ibid; also Navy Office to Registrar Births Deaths and Marriages 25 September 1944
128	NA Navy Department Series 1 6/1/25 'Conditions of Transfer of Gambia', Navy Office Wgtn to Minister of Defence 1 December 1943.

Chapter Four: Guadalcanal to Green Islands

1	D. M. Skinner Collection, H. Skinner letter home, 25 November 1943
2	Matthew Wright, *Italian Odyssey*, Reed, Auckland 2003, pp. 12-14.

3   Mayer (ed), p. 172.
4   *Documents*, Vol. III, Letter from Major-General Barrowclough to the Prime Minister, p. 416.
5   Matthew Wright, *Desert Duel*, p. 68.
6   Morgan, 11 January 1943.
7   D. M. Skinner Collection, H. Skinner letter home, 25 November 1943.
8   Op cit, 10 December 1943
9   Ibid.
10 WTu MS Papers 3907 Waterman Family Collection, letter to 'Dear Dad & All', 3 October 1943
11 RNZN Navy Museum Oral History, J. L. W. Salter
12 Ibid.
13 Gillespie, p. 162.
14 D. M. Skinner Collection, H. Skinner letter home, 7 November 1943
15 Gillespie, p. 162.
16 Ibid, p. 124.
17 D. M. Skinner Collection, H. Skinner letter home, 7 November 1943
18 Gillespie, p. 118.
19 D. M. Skinner Collection, H. Skinner letter home, 7 November 1943. The men were forbidden to mention the name of the anti-malarial drug in letters.
20 — *Pacific Saga*, Reed, Wellington, n.d. p. 61
21 Gillespie, p. 162.
22 Ibid.
23 WTu MS Papers 3907 Waterman Family Collection, letter to 'Dear Dad & All', 20 September 1943
24 D. M. Skinner Collection, H. Skinner letter home, 7 November 1943
25 *Documents*, Vol. III, Barrowclough to Army HQ, Wellington, 20 September 1943, p. 410.
26 D. M. Skinner Collection, H. Skinner letter home, 25 November 1943. This *ad-hoc* unit was also known as the Forward Maintenance Centre, see Gillespie p. 123, n. 1.
27 D. M. Skinner Collection, H. Skinner letter home, 25 November 1943.
28 Op cit, H. Skinner letter home, 7 November 1943
29 WTu Ref MS-Papers-6566 Excerpts from the diaries of T L Thomas/transcribed by Nan Thomas.
3   WTu MS-Papers-2001-008-054, Thompson, Eric Hardisty, 1922-2000: Charlie Nicholson's Green Islands Story
31 *Documents*, Vol. III, Memorandum from Major-General Barrowclough to Army Headquarters (Wellington), 20 September 1943, p. 407.
32 Ibid
33 — *The 35th Battalion*, p. 41.
34 Ibid, p. 40
35 *Documents*, Vol. III, Letter from Major-General Barrowclough to the Prime Minister, p. 418.
36 Ibid p. 419.
37 *Documents*, Vol. III, Memorandum from Major-General Barrowclough to Army Headquarters (Wellington), 20 September 1943, p. 407. 408.
38 *The 35th Battalion*, p. 42.
39 *Documents*, Vol. III, Letter from Major-General Barrowclough to the Prime Minister, p. 419.
40 WTu Ref MS-Papers-6566 Excerpts from the diaries of T L Thomas/transcribed by Nan Thomas, Thomas, Trevor Lloyd, 1919 - World War Two diaries and scrapbook.
41 Ibid.
42 *The 35th Battalion*, p. 47.
43 Ibid, p. 48.
44 Ibid, p. 49.
45 WTu Ref MS-Papers-6566 Excerpts from the diaries of T L Thomas/transcribed by Nan Thomas, Thomas, Trevor Lloyd, 1919 - World War Two diaries and scrapbook.
46 Ibid, p. 74.
47 — *Pacific Saga*, p. 74.
48 *Documents*, Vol. III, HQ 3 Division to Army HQ (Wellington), 9 October 1943, p. 412.

49   Gillespie, p. 138.
50   WTu Ref MS-Papers-6566 Excerpts from the diaries of T L Thomas/transcribed by Nan Thomas, Thomas, Trevor Lloyd, 1919 - World War Two diaries and scrapbook.
51   *Documents*, Vol. III, Letter from Major-General Barrowclough to the Prime Minister, p. 420.
52   Op cit, Letter from Major-General Barrowclough to the Prime Minister, 31 December 1943, p. 422
53   Barber, p. 133.
54   *Documents*, Vol. III, Letter from Major-General Barrowclough to the Prime Minister, 31 December 1943, p. 421.
55   Ibid.
56   Ibid, p. 422.
57   Crawford, p. 153; citing NA WAII Z/151, 1/23, Barrowclough to Puttick 30 November 1943,
58   Gillespie, p. 155, n. 6.
59   Ibid, p. 155.
60   — *The MMG's*, A H & A W Reed, Wellington, n.d., p. 215.
61   Ross, pp. 204-205
62   *Documents*, Vol. III, Letter from Major-General Barrowclough to the Prime Minister, 31 December 1943, p. 422.
63   Gillespie, p. 151.
64   Ibid, p. 160.
65   *Documents*, Vol. III, Letter from Major-General Barrowclough to the Prime Minister, 31 December 1943, p. 423.
66   Gillespie, p. 156.
67   *Documents*, Vol. III, Letter from Major-General Barrowclough to the Prime Minister, 31 December 1943, p. 422.
68   Gillespie, p. 158. See also *Documents*, Vol. III, Letter from Major-General Barrowclough to the Prime Minister, 31 December 1943, p. 422, citing 39 dead and 146 wounded.
69   WTu Ref MS-Papers-6566 Excerpts from the diaries of T L Thomas/transcribed by Nan Thomas, Thomas, Trevor Lloyd, 1919 - World War Two diaries and scrapbook.
70   D. M. Skinner Collection, H. Skinner, letter home 9 January 1944.
71   Ross, p. 208.
72   D. M. Skinner Collection, Ted Skinner, letter home 21 January 1944.
73   Op cit, 14 January 1944.
74   Op cit, 8 February 1944.
75   — *The 35th Battalion*, p. 61.
76   Ibid, p. 63.
77   Ibid.
78   — *Pacific Kiwis*, p. 86.
79   — *The 35th Battalion*, p. 63.
80   — *Pacific Kiwis*, p. 87.
81   NA WAII Series 9 File S1, Major-General Barrowclough (Personal), Barrowclough to Puttick, 6 January 1944.
82   WTu ref 76-106 Lucas, Jim, fl. 1944, letter to A M describing the US Marine landing at Tarawa.
83   NA WAII Series 9 File S1, Major-General Barrowclough (Personal), Barrowclough to Puttick, 6 January 1944.
84   Ibid.
85   Ibid.
86   NA WAII Series 9 File S1, Major-General Barrowclough (Personal), Barrowclough to Puttick, 17 February 1944.
87   Gillespie, pp. 171-172.
88   — *Pacific Kiwis*, p. 90.
89   Ibid, p. 92.
90   Ibid, p. 93.
91   Gillespie, pp. 175-176.
92   — *Pacific Kiwis*, p. 91.

93   Ibid, p. 94.
94   D. M. Skinner Collection, H. Skinner, letter home 4 April 1944.
95   Op cit, H. Skinner, letter home 18 April 1944.
96   Gillespie, p. 176.
97   D. M. Skinner Collection, H. Skinner, letter home 7 April 1944.
98   Gillespie, p. 179.
99   WTu Ref MS-Papers-6566 Excerpts from the diaries of T L Thomas/transcribed by Nan Thomas, Thomas, Trevor Lloyd, 1919 - World War Two diaries and scrapbook.
100 Ibid.
101 — *Pacific Kiwis*, p. 107.
102 Ibid.
103 WTu Ref MS-Papers-6566 Excerpts from the diaries of T L Thomas/transcribed by Nan Thomas, Thomas, Trevor Lloyd, 1919 - World War Two diaries and scrapbook.
104 Ibid.
105 Ibid.
106 Ibid.
107 Gillespie, p. 187.
108 WTu MS-Papers-2001-008-054, Thompson, Eric Hardisty, 1922-2000: Charlie Nicholson's Green Islands Story
109 D. M. Skinner Collection, H. Skinner, letter home 14 March 1944.
110 WTu MS-Papers-2001-008-054, Thompson, Eric Hardisty, 1922-2000: Charlie Nicholson's Green Islands Story
111 Ibid.
112 WTu Ref MS-Papers-6566 Excerpts from the diaries of T L Thomas/transcribed by Nan Thomas, Thomas, Trevor Lloyd, 1919 - World War Two diaries and scrapbook.
113 Ross Galbreath 'Dr Marsden and Admiral Halsey' in John Crawford (ed) *Kia Kaha*, pp. 252-263.

Chapter Five: Tides of War
1   *Documents*, Vol. III, Deputy Prime Minister to Admiral Halsey, p. 430.
2   Matthew Wright *Italian Odyssey*, Reed 2003, p. 117.
3   Op cit, The Hon W. Nash (Noumea) to the Prime Minister, 31 December 1943.
4   *Documents*, II, letter from the Hon. W. Nash, New Zealand Minister at Washington, to President Roosevelt, 24 January 1944, p. 333.
5   Op cit, New Zealand Minister (Washington) to the Prime Minister of New Zealand (Canberra), 14 January 1944, p. 329.
6   Ibid, see also Churchill, V, p. 398
7   *Documents*, II, The Hon. W. Nash (Washington) to the Prime Minister of New Zealand, 2 February 1944, p. 336.
8   Gillespie, p. 195.
9   *Documents*, II, The Hon W. E. Nash (London) to the Prime Minister, 27 February 1944, p. 340.
10   Matthew Wright, *Italian Odyssey*, Reed, Auckland 2003, esp. Chapters 2-3.
11   *Documents*, II, The Hon W. E. Nash (London) to the Prime Minister, 27 February 1944, p. 345
12   Cited in M. P. Lissington *New Zealand and the United States* p 83. It was signed on 21 January.
13   Cited in Gillespie, Appendix VIII, p. 347.
14   Ibid, pp 347, 352.
15   NA WAII Series 9 File S1, Major-General Barrowclough (Personal), Barrowclough to Puttick, 4 March 1944.
16   Gillespie p. 197
17   *Documents*, Vol. III, The Prime Minister of New Zealand to the Hon. W. Nash (London), 1 April 1944, p. 344.
18   Gillespie, p. 197.
19   Op cit, H. Skinner, letter home 12 April 1944.
20   WTu Ref MS-Papers-6566 Excerpts from the diaries of T L Thomas/transcribed by Nan Thomas, Thomas, Trevor Lloyd, 1919 - World War Two diaries and scrapbook.

21 Gillespie, p. 199.
22 *Documents*, Vol. III, General Freyberg to Prime Minister, 2 April 1944, p. 346.
23 Matthew Wright *Italian Odyssey*, Reed, Auckland 2003, p. 117.
24 *Documents, III.*, p 206
25 Op cit, pp 208-09
26 Op cit p 211.
27 *Documents*, Vol. III, Army Headquarters to Admiral Newton, p. 444.
28 Op cit, Letter from Major-General Barrowclough to the Acting Prime Minister, 30 June 1944, p. 441.
29 Op cit, Prime Minister to Major-General Barrowclough, 30 August 1944, p. 453.
30 Matthew Wright, *Italian Odyssey*, p. xx.
31 *Documents*, Vol. III, Recommendation by General Barrowclough, Brigadier Conway and Mr H L Beckett for relief of long-service personnel.
32 *Documents* III, War Cabinet Minute, p. 456.
33 Op cit, Special Order of the Day by Major-General Barrowclough to 3rd New Zealand Divison, pp. 456-457.
34 Matthew Wright, *Italian Odyssey*, pp. xx.
35 NA AIR 149/1 No. 14 Squadron Operations Record Book April 1942- September 1945,
36 *Ibid*, 31 December 1944.
37 NA AIR 100/8 Air Vice Marshall Isitt Correspondence, 5 March 1945.
38 NA AIR 149/1 No. 14 Squadron Operations Record Book April 1942- September 1945, 5 April 1945.
39 *Ibid*, 26 April 1945.
40 Roskill, III, p. 346.
41 Winston Churchill, *The Second World War*, Vol. V, Cassell & Co., London, 1952, p. 494.
42 Cited in ibid, p. 495.
43 Cited in ibid, p. 511.
44 Roskill, Vol. III, p. 348.
45 WTu MS Papers 2297, Mackie, R. F., letters and correspondence, letter home 6 May 1944.
46 Bennett, p. 220.
47 Ibid, p. 234.
48 Ibid, p. 240-41. See also Garzke and Dulin, pp. 107-151.
49 Cunningham, p. 606.
50 Richard Jackson 'That Offensive Spirit', *New Zealand Defence Quarterly*, Spring 1995, p. 31.
51 Waters, p. 375.
52 RNZN Museum Oral History Chief Electrician R. B. Harvey B.E.M., RNZN (Rtd)
53 Waters, p. 383.
54 Ibid, p. 385.
55 RNZN Museum Oral History Chief Electrician R. B. Harvey B.E.M., RNZN (Rtd)
56 WTu Ms-Papers-2297, Mackie, R. F., letters and correspondence, letter home 20 July 1945.
57 Ibid.
58 RNZN Museum Oral History Chief Electrician R. B. Harvey B.E.M., RNZN (Rtd)
59 RNZN Museum Oral History J. L. W. Salter, BEM, MID, RNZNVR (Rtd).
60 Matthew Wright, *Italian Odyssey*, Reed, Auckland 2003, pp. 146-156.
61 *Documents*, Vol. III, Prime Minister of the United Kingdom to the Prime Minister of New Zealand, 18 September 1944, p. 462.
62 Op cit, Prime Minister of the United Kingdom to the Prime Minister of New Zealand, 27 January 1945, p. 463.
63 Ibid, p. 464.
64 Ibid.
65 NA WAII 8/78 Future Employment and Problems of Change-Over, Fraser to Freyberg 3 February 1945.
66 Ibid.
67 Op cit, Nash to Freyberg, 8 April 1945.
68 Op cit, Freyberg to Nash, 11 April 1945.

69   *Documents*, Vol. III, W. Nash to the Prime Minister (London), 7 April 1945, p. 467.
70   Op cit, General Freyberg to the Acting Prime Minister, 11 April 1945, p. 468.
71   Op cit, General Freyberg to the Minister of Defence, 15 May 1945, p. 473.
72   NA WAII 8/78 Future Employment and Problems of Change-Over, Leese to Freyberg, 25 May 1945.
73   *Documents*, Vol. III, New Zealand Military Liaison Officer (London) to the Prime Minister of New Zealand (San Francisco), 21 May 1943, p. 476.
74   Op cit, New Zealand Military Liaison Officer (London) to the Prime Minister of New Zealand (San Francisco), 21 May 1943, p. 477; General Freyberg to the Acting Prime Minister, 27 May 1943, p. 477, 479-480.
75   Op cit, Prime Minister of the United Kingdom to the Prime Minister of New Zealand, 5 July 1945, p. 488.
76   Op cit, Prime Minister of New Zealand to the Prime Minister of the United Kingdom, 14 July 1945, p. 489.
77   NA WAII 8/79 Future Employment and Problems of Change-Over, File 2, Fraser to Freyberg, 6 August 1945; Freyberg to Fraser, 7 August 1945. See also Matthew Wright *Blue Water Kiwis*, Reed NZ Ltd, Auckland p. 143.
78   *Documents*, Vol. III, General Freyberg (London) to the Prime Minister, 7 August 1945, p. 495.
79   Richard B. Frank, 'No Bomb: no end, the Operation Olympic Disaster, Japan 1945', in Robert Cowley (ed) *What if? 2 — Historians imagine what might have been*, Berkeley, New York, 2001, p. 370. See also *Documents*, Vol. III, SSDA to the acting Prime Minister of New Zealand, 6 May 1945, pp. 497-498.
80   Frank, p. 370.
81   Also given as 1 November, see Frank p. 372.
82   *Documents*, Vol. III, Prime Minister of the United Kingdom to the Prime Minister of New Zealand, 31 July 1945, p. 501.
83   Frank, p. 375.
84   Winston Churchill, *The Second World War*, Vol. VI, Cassell & Co., London, 1954, p. 552.
85   Frank, p. 376.
86   Ibid, pp. 380-381.
87   Owen Wilkes 'New Zealand and the atom bomb' in John Crawford (ed) *Kia Kaha*, pp. 264-275.
88   Mayer (ed), p. 246
89   Churchill, *The Second World War*, Vol. VI, p. 553.
90   *Documents*, Vol. III, SSDA to the Prime Minister of New Zealand, 7 August 1945, p. 502.
91   Report of the New Zealand Naval Board for the period 1st April 1945 to 31st March 1946, p. 3.
92   *Ibid*, p. 3.
93   NA Navy Department 67/16 HMSNZ *Gambia* Ship's Log, August 1945, entry 27 August 1945.
94   RNZN Museum Oral History Chief Electrician R. B. Harvey B.E.M., RNZN (Rtd).
95   Churchill, *The Second World War*, Vol. VI, p. 479.

Epilogue: The Legacy of War
1   Richard Jackson 'That Offensive Spirit', *New Zealand Defence Quarterly*, Spring 1995, p. 34.
2   Matthew Wright *Kiwi Air Power*, pp. 125-129, 157-160 169-172.
3   Cited in Gillespie p. 107.
4   Cited in ibid, p. 103.
5   See also Matthew Wright *A Near-Run Affair — New Zealanders in the Battle for Crete, 1941*, Reed, Auckland 2000, pp. 100-101, 109; Matthew Wright, *Blue Water Kiwis*, pp. 108-109.
6   F. L. W. Wood, *Political and External Affairs*, Historical Publications Branch, Wellington, 1958, title of Chapter 26.
7   *Documents*, Vol. III, Prime Minister of the United Kingdom to the Prime Minister of New Zealand, 15 August 1945, p. 508.
8   W. D. McIntyre 'Peter Fraser's Commonwealth: New Zealand and the Origins of the New Commonwealth in the 1940s', in *New Zealand in World Affairs*, Vol. 1, Price Milburn for the New Zealand Institute of International Affairs, Wellington 1977, pp. 9-36; Wood, pp. 370-384;

Michael Ashby 'Fraser's Foreign Policy' in Margaret Clark (ed) *Peter Fraser: Master Politician*, The Dunmore Press, Palmerston North, 1998.
9   Cited in McIntyre, p. 40.
10   Cited in ibid, p. 39.
11   Ashby p. 189.
12   F. L. W. Wood 'Foreign Policy 1945-1951' in *New Zealand in World Affairs*, Vol. 1, Price Milburn for the New Zealand Institute of International Affairs, Wellington 1977, p. 119.

Glossary

25-pounder	New Zealand artillery piece firing a 25-pound weight shell.
Asdic	Acronym for the British underwater submarine detection system.
Bofors	A 20-mm anti-aircraft machine gun.
Cactus	Allied code-name for Guadalcanal.
Construction Battalion	(CB) US term for field engineers, also nicknamed 'Seabees'.
Necal	Military abbreviation for New Caledonia.
Co-Prosperity Sphere	Name of the Japanese empire planned in 1940.
3 NZ Division	Third New Zealand Division.
2 NZEFIP	Second New Zealand Expeditionary Force in the Pacific — the force New Zealand sent to New Caledonia in 1942, including combat troops, base units, administrators, hospitals, training establishments and supply companies. 3 NZ Division was the combat component.
army	A formation normally comprising two or more corps.
battalion	A formation normally comprising three or four companies.
Bren	The standard British light machine gun, originally the Brno (BR) ZB-26, further developed by Enfield (EN).
brigade	A formation normally comprising three or four battalions.
brigade group	A brigade with the addition of other units for specialised tasks.
Bofors	A 40-mm anti-aircraft machine gun.
company	A unit comprising three or four platoons.
Construction Battalion (CB)	US term for an engineering unit of the US Marines, also nicknamed Seabee.
corps	A formation usually comprising two or more divisions.

division	A formation normally comprising three brigades and associated forces.
EPS	Emergency Precautions Service, a civilian emergency organisation set up in New Zealand after the 1931 Hawke's Bay earthquake.
GSO1	General Service Officer, an administrative post. Also GSO2, GSO3 etc.
GOC	General Officer Commanding; New Zealand's two front-line GOCs were Lieutenant-General Sir Bernard Freyberg (2 NZ Division) and Major-General Harold Barrowclough (3 NZ Division).
New Zealand Naval Division	The New Zealand-funded branch of the Royal Navy that became the RNZN in 1941.
Oerlikon	A 20-mm heavy machine gun.
platoon	An infantry unit comprising two or three sections, normally 20–25 men.
RNZAF	Royal New Zealand Air Force, formed in 1937.
RNZN	Royal New Zealand Navy, formed in 1941.
Ultra	The British system for decrypting German ENIGMA code messages.
Seabee	*See* Construction Battalion.
Section	The basic infantry unit.
Task force	US military terminology for a naval force set up for a specific purpose.
USAAF	United States Army Air Force. US military air power did not become a separate service until after the Second World War.
USMC	United States Marine Corps.
Universal Carrier	Also known as a Bren Gun Carrier; a British multi-purpose, open-topped tracked vehicle principally designed to carry troops and weaponry into the battlefield.
Valentine	Mk III Infantry Tank, a slow, well-armoured and lightly armed tank developed by the British. Although obsolete in the European theatre by 1943–44, it was still used by the New Zealanders in the Pacific, where there was almost no tank opposition.

Bibliography

Primary sources

Alexander Turnbull Library (WTu)
Micro MS 0842 John Edward Morgan diary Sept 1942–April 1943
MS Papers 1390 J.L. Martin collection
MS Papers 1437 Haldane collection
MS Papers 1494 Neal Family collection
MS Papers 1823 H. Gladstone Hill collection
MS Papers 1912 John Martin collection
MS Papers 2183 Hon F. Jones collection
MS Papers 2446 H.G. Miller collection
MS Papers ACC 91-326 Henderson collection
MS-Papers-7417-3 Richard Andrew — letters to his family and other papers
MS-Papers-6566 Excerpts from the diaries of T.L. Thomas, transcribed by Nan Thomas
MS-Papers-76-106 Lucas, Jim, fl. 1944, letter to A.M. describing the US Marine landing at Tarawa
MS-Papers-2001-008-054 Thompson, Eric Hardisty, 1922–2000: Papers. Charlie Thompson's Green Islands story
MS-Papers 2297, Mackie, R.F., Letters and Correspondence
MS-Papers-7417-3, Andrew family: Papers, Richard Andrew, letters to his family and other papers
MS-Papers-3907, Waterman Family Collection.

Archives New Zealand/Te Whare Tohu Tuhituhinga O Aotearoa
Air Department
Series 1, 102/5/1 Misc. Malayan Campaign — RNZAF Official

Series 1, 106/2/1 Scale of Attack on New Zealand
Series 100, 8 Air Vice Marshal Isitt Correspondence 1943–45
Series 118, 52 War History narrative of life in Santo, Base Report; Appendix B1 RNZAF Station Espiritu Santo
Series 118, 57 No.1 Aerodrome Construction Unit
Series 128, 1 COMAIRSOLS: Strike Command War Diary Nov 1943–Mar 1944
Series 139, /9 No.3 (BR) Sqn — Operational Sorties Jan 1943–Jan 1944.
Series 149, 1 No. 14 Sqn Operations Record Book April 1942–Sept 1945
Seres 150, 12 Personal narrative of experiences with 15 Squadron 1942–43 by B.A. Berry 1942–43
Series 150, 13 Diary and narrative of F/S J.J. Mackie of Waipukurau; 14 Squadron in Tonga and Santo, 18 Squadron in Solomons Oct–Nov 1943

Navy Department
Series 1, 6/1/25 'Conditions of Transfer of Gambia'
Series 1, 6/35/2 Ships and repairs: Loss of HMNZS *Moa* due to enemy action
Series 1, 10/7 CID Reports August 1922, Washington Treaty
Series 1,16/8/35 Operations: HMNZS *Monowai*, encounter with submarine and aircraft, January 1942
Series 1,16/8/40 Operations: HMNZS *Achilles*, encounter with Japanese dive-bomber, January 1943
Series 1,16/8/43 Operations: HMNZS *Leander*, encounter with Japanese naval forces, Kula Gulf, July 1943
Series 1,16/8/44 Operations: Report of submarine in Cook Strait, November 1943
Series 1,62/27/6 Ships and repairs: HMS *Achilles* — report of damage
Series 67, 16 HMNZS *Gambia* Ship's Log, August 1945

External Affairs Department
Series 1, 85/1/22 General 'Japanese Plans for the Invasion of New Zealand', Part 1
Series 1, 86/27/10, Verbatim Report of Proceedings

War Archives, World War Two
Series 9, S1, Major-General Barrowclough (Personal)
Series 8, 78, Future Employment and Problems of Change-Over, File 1.
Series 8, 79, Future Employment and Problems of Change-Over, File 2.

National Library
Appendices to the Journal of the House of Representatives
New Zealand Parliamentary Debates

Private papers, photographic collections and correspondence
Nolan Wynn
Howard Skinner

Published Primary Sources
Fairbrother, M.C. (ed) *Documents Relating to New Zealand's Participation in the Second World War*, Vol. III, War History Branch, Department of Internal Affairs, Wellington, 1963.
In Time of War: Selections from the Wartime addresses of the Rt. Hon. Peter Fraser, Government Print, Wellington, 1946.
Kay, Robin (ed), *The Australian New Zealand Agreement 1944*, Historical Publications Branch, Government Print, Wellington, 1972.
Kimball, Warren F. (ed) *Churchill & Roosevelt, The Complete Correspoondence*, Princeton University Press, Princeton, New Jersey, 1984.
New Zealand Foreign Policy Statements and Documents, 1943–1957, Foreign Affairs, Government Print, Wellington, 1972.

Secondary Sources

Barber, Laurie and Henshall, Ken, *The Last War of Empires — Japan and the Pacific War, 1941–45*, David Bateman, Auckland 1999.
Bennett, Neville, 'Consultation or information? Great Britain, The Dominions, and the Renewal of the Anglo-Japanese Alliance, 1911', *New Zealand Journal of History*, Vol 4, No. 2, October 1970.
Bioletti, Harry, *The Yanks are Coming — The American invasion of New Zealand 1942–1944*, Century Hutchinson, Auckland, 1999.
Bridge, Carl, 'Australia, New Zealand and Allied grand strategy 1941–43', in Crawford, John (ed), *Kia Kaha, New Zealand in the Second World War*, Oxford University Press, Melbourne, 2002.
Callahan, Raymond, 'The Illusion of Security: Singapore 1919–1942', *Journal of Contemporary History*, Vol. 9, No. 2, April 1976.
Central Office of Information, *Among Those Present — The official story of the Pacific islands at war*, HM Stationery Office, London, 1946.

Clark, Margaret (ed), *Peter Fraser, Master Politician*, Dunmore Press, Palmerston North, 1998.

Churchill, Winston S., *The Second World War*, Vols I–VI, Cassell & Co, London, 1948–1954.

Conly, Geoff, *Wattie's — The First Fifty Years*, J. Wattie Canneries, Hastings, 1984.

Cook, Theodore F., Jr, 'Our Midway Disaster' in Robert Cowley (ed), *What If? —Military Historians imagine what might have been*, Pan, London, 2001.

Crawford, John, *New Zealand's Pacific Frontline, Guadalcanal — Solomon Islands Campaign 1942–45*, NZDF, Wellington, 1992.

Crawford, John, 'A Campaign on two fronts: Barrowclough in the Pacific', in Crawford, John (ed), *Kia Kaha, New Zealand in the Second World War*, Oxford University Press, Melbourne, 2002, reprint.

Dalziel, R.M., *The Origins of New Zealand Diplomacy*, Price Millburn for the Victoria University Press, Wellington, 1975.

Dixon, Norman, *On the Psychology of Military Incompetence*, Pimlico, London, 1976.

Frank, Richard B. 'No Bomb: no end, the Operation Olympic Disaster, Japan 1945', in Robert Cowley (ed), *What if? 2 — Historians imagine what might have been*, Berkeley, New York, 2001.

Galbreath, Ross, 'Dr Marsden and Admiral Halsey' in John Crawford (ed), *Kia Kaha, New Zealand in the Second World War*, Oxford University Press, Melbourne 2002, reprint.

Garzke, William H. and Dulin, Robert O., *British, Soviet, French and Dutch Battleships of World War II*, Jane's Publishing Company, London, 1980.

Garzke, William H. and Dulin, Robert O., *American Battleships of World War II*, Jane's Publishing Company, London, 1976.

Gillespie, Oliver A., *The Pacific*, War History Branch, Department of Internal Affairs, Wellington, 1952.

Gordon, B.K., *New Zealand becomes a Pacific Power*, University of Chicago Press, Chicago, 1960.

Gowen, R.J., 'British Legerdemain at the 1911 Imperial Conference: The Dominions, Defence Planning and the Renewal of the Anglo-Japanese Alliance', *Journal of Modern History*, Vol. 52 No. 3, August 1980.

Harrison, Paul, Brian Lockstone and Andy Anderson, *The Golden Age of New Zealand Flying Boats*, Random House, Auckland 1997.

Hattendorf, John B., 'American strategies in the Pacific war', in Crawford, John (ed), *Kia Kaha, New Zealand in the Second World War*, Oxford University

Press, Melbourne, 2002, reprint.

Henderson, John, Keith Jackson and Richard Kennaway (eds), *Beyond New Zealand — The Foreign Policy of a Small State*, Methuen New Zealand, Auckland, 1980.

Jablonski, Edward, *A Pictorial History of the World War II Years*, Wings Books, New York, 1977.

Jackson, Richard, 'That Offensive Spirit', *New Zealand Defence Quarterly*, Spring 1995.

Kennedy, Paul M., *Strategy and Diplomacy, 1870–1946*, Fontana, London, 1984.

———— *The Rise and Fall of British Naval Mastery*, Allen Lane, London, 1976.

Larkin, T.C. (ed), *New Zealand's External Relations*, OUP, Pegasus Press, Christchurch, 1962.

Lissington, M.P. *New Zealand and the United States, 1840–1944*, Government Print, Wellington, 1972.

———— *New Zealand and Japan, 1900–1941*, New Zealand Government Printer, Wellington 1972.

Mansergh, Nicholas, *Survey of British Commonwealth Affairs — Problems of External Policy 1931–1939*, Oxford University Press, London, 1952.

Martin, John E. 'Total war? The National Service Department and New Zealand's manpower crisis of 1942', in Crawford, John (ed), *Kia Kaha, New Zealand in the Second World War*, Oxford University Press, Melbourne, 2002, reprint.

McCarthy, Frank, *Singapore Harriers, Pictorial Record of the RNZAF No.1 Aerodrome Construction Squadron, Malaya 1941–42*, unpub., Auckland.

McDougall, R.J., *New Zealand Naval Vessels*, GP Books, Wellington, 1989.

Meaney, Neville, *The Search for Security in the Pacific*, Vol I, Sydney University Press, Sydney, 1976.

Monger, G.W., *The End of Isolation*, Thomas Nelson & Sons, London, 1963.

Moore, John Hammond, *The American Alliance — Australia, New Zealand and the United States 1940–1970*, Cassell Australia, Melbourne, 1970.

Nish, I.H., 'Australia and the Anglo-Japanese Alliance', *Australian Journal of Politics and History*, Vol. 9, No. 2, November 1963.

———— *Alliance in Decline*, The Athlone Press, University of London, London, 1966, 1968 reprint.

———— *The Anglo Japanese Alliance*, The Athlone Press, University of London, London, 1966, 1968 reprint.

Priday, H.E. Lewis, *The War from Coconut Square*, A.H. & A.W. Reed,

Wellington, 1945.

Ross, J.M.S., *Royal New Zealand Air Force*, War History Branch, Dept. Internal Affairs, Wellington, 1955.

Stevens, David (ed), *Maritime Power in the Twentieth Century — The Australian Experience*, Allen and Unwin, St Leonards, 1998.

Storry, Richard, *A History of Modern Japan*, Penguin, London, 1960.

Tarling, Nicholas, *A Sudden Rampage — The Japanese occupation of Southeast Asia, 1941–45*, Hurst & Co., London, 2001.

Templeton, Malcolm, *Ties of Blood and Empire*, Auckland University Press, Auckland 1994.

Third Division Histories Committee, *Tanks, MMGs & Ordnance*, A.H. & A.W. Reed, Wellington, n.d.

—— *Pacific Kiwis*, A.H. & A.W. Reed, Wellington, n.d.

—— *Pacific Saga*, A.H. & A.W. Reed, Wellington, n.d.

—— *The 35th Battalion*, A.H. & A.W. Reed, Wellington, n.d.

Thompson, Roger C., *Australian Imperialism in the Pacific: The Expansionist Era*, Melbourne University Press, Melbourne, 1980.

Towle, P.A., 'The Effect of the Russo-Japanese War on British Naval Policy', *Mariner's Mirror*, Vol. 60, No. 4, November 1970.

Tsuji, Masanobu, *Singapore — The Japanese Version*, trans. Margaret E. Lake, Ure Smith, Sydney, 1960.

Waters, S.D., *The Royal New Zealand Navy*, War History Branch, Department of Internal Affairs, Wellington, 1956.

Wilkes, Owen, 'New Zealand and the atom bomb' in John Crawford (ed), *Kia Kaha, New Zealand in the Second World War*, Oxford University Press, Melbourne, 2002, reprint.

Wright, Matthew, *Kiwi Air Power — The History of the RNZAF*, Reed, Auckland, 1998.

—— *Blue Water Kiwis — New Zealand's Naval Story*, Reed, Auckland, 2001.

—— *Desert Duel — New Zealand's North African War 1940–43*, Reed, Auckland, 2002.

—— *Italian Odyssey — New Zealanders in the Battle for Italy 1943–45*, Reed, Auckland, 2003.

Index

A
Achilles, HMNZS (after November 1941), 15, 38, 56, 58, 60, 65, 98, 100-102, 120, 130
Ainsworth, Admiral W. L., 62
Aleutians, 2, 38
Allingham, Lieutenant J. D., 108
Andaman Islands, 10, 22, 97
Anti-Comintern Pact, 8
Anzio, 97
Aotea Quay, 25, 44
Arafura Sea, 10, 22
Arbutus, HMNZS (ship), 102
Atebrin (anti-malarial), 68, 69, 72
Atomic bomb, 1, 106, 107
Aylward, W. T. A., 86

B
Balfour, Squadron Leader R. H., 81
Balikpapan, 23
Bangkok, 10, 14, 22
Barrowclough, Major-General Harold, 46-48, 50, 67, 69, 70-72, 76, 77, 79-83, 86, 88-89, 90, 93-95, 118, 119, 121-124, 128, 130, 132
Bataan Peninsula, 23
Bay of Bengal, 97
Belgrave, Lieutenant C., 61
Besara River, 78
Biloa, 70, 71
Bockett, H. L., 95

Bougainville, 10, 22, 24, 57, 60, 61, 67-69, 76, 77, 80, 82, 83, 90, 95-97
Bourail, 49, 50
Brewster Buffalo, 15
Bridson, Lieutenant-Commander Gordon, 59
Brisbane, 2, 37
Burma, 10, 11, 22, 23, 32, 38, 66, 76, 97, 103, 104

C

Calcutta, 10, 22
Cambodia ,14
Canberra, 35, 36, 92-94, 110, 123
Cape Esperance, 59
Caroline Islands, 2, 23, 62, 76
Cassino, 95
Chance-Vought F4U Corsair, 96, 107
Chirovanga, 57, 60, 68
Choiseul, 57, 60, 66, 68, 77, 82, 83, 96
Christchurch, 26, 30, 133
Churchill, Sir Winston S., 4, 9-15, 18, 20, 25, 28-31, 34-36, 66, 92, 97, 103, 104, 107, 108, 110, 113-115, 117, 123-125, 131, 132
Cochrane, Air Vice-Marshal Ralph, 8
Conway, Brigadier A. E., 95, 113, 124
Corbett, Flying Officer D. A., 96
Cornwall, Lieutenant-Colonel F. C., 83, 86, 88
Corrigedor, 23
Cowan, Sergeant W. A., 77
Cowan's 77
Crichton, Squadron Leader A., 54
Cunningham, Admiral Sir Andrew, 100, 124
Curtin, John, 34, 35
Curtis P-40 Kittyhawk, 43, 54, 71, 78, 81, 82

D

Darwin, 2, 18, 24
De Havilland Vincent, 52
Deverell, Captain G. R., 26, 27
Dixon, Peter, 101, 115, 132
Dumbo (term for any air-sea rescue aircraft), 55, 60, 96

Dutch East Indies, 2, 13, 14, 18, 23, 76, 98, 114, 132

E
Easton, Laurie, 56
Efate, 53, 55
Eisenhower, General Dwight D., 36, 37
Electra, HMS (ship), 17
Emirau 90, 95, 102
Emperor Hirohito, 107
Eniwetok, 10, 22
Erskine M. Phelps, USS (ship), 60
Espiritu Santo, 45, 52, 53, 55, 56, 58, 61, 64, 119, 130

F
Fairmile launch, 65
Fiji 2, 8, 9, 24, 26-29, 32-34, 36-38, 43, 44, 45, 48, 52, 61, 72, 91, 104.
Florida Island, 77
Formosa (Taiwan), 10, 22, 100
FPDA (Five Power Defence Arrangement), 112
France 8, 9, 11, 12, 106
Fraser, Peter, 3, 4, 9-13, 15, 18, 25, 28, 29, 31, 35-37, 42, 44, 48, 67, 77, 91-95, 100, 103, 104, 110, 111, 113, 114, 116, 124-126, 131, 132
Fremantle, 27
Freyberg, Lieutenant-General Sir Bernard, 94, 95, 103-105, 114, 116, 124, 125, 128
Fumota Airfield, 54

G
Gallipoli 77
Gambia, HMNZS (ship), 65, 97, 98, 100-102, 107, 108, 120, 125, 130
Ghormley, Rear-Admiral Robert, 37, 42-45
Grumman F6 Hellcat, 98
Guadalcanal, 2, 41, 44-47, 52, 55, 57-61, 65-72, 76, 77, 83, 89, 120, 127, 132
Guam, 10, 22, 23, 98
Gudsell, Flying Officer G. E., 55

H

Hamaguchi, Osachi, 7
Hamakaze, IJN (ship), 62
Hanoi, 10, 22
Hawaii, 2, 6, 34
Hawke's Bay, 30, 50, 116, 128
Henderson Field, 55, 59, 60, 129, 133
Hiroshima, 10, 22, 107
Hokkaido 10, 22
Honolulu, 58, 62, 63
Honshu, 10, 22, 105

I

Implacable, HMS (ship), 101
Indefatigable, HMS (ship), 107
India, 10, 22, 23, 32, 38
Indo-China, 10-13, 22
Indomitable, HMS (ship), 100
Isitt, Marshal Leonard, 96, 108, 124, 130
Ito, Lieutenant Isumo, 27

J

Jacquinot Bay, 95, 102
Japan 1-15, 18, 20, 22-27, 29-34, 36, 38-40, 45, 57, 60-62, 68, 76, 77, 88, 93, 97, 99-101, 103-109, 111, 113, 114, 117, 125, 131-134
Java, 10, 18, 20-24, 28, 38
Jayforce 109
Jintsu, IJN (ship), 62
Johore, 18-20

K

Kabien, 95
Kallang, 19, 109
Kavieng 10, 22, 82, 90, 92, 95
Kendari, 23
Kidson, Squadron Leader C. J., 52
Kieta Roncador Reef, 57, 68
Kiritak, 20

Kolombangara 60, 62, 66, 70, 76
Konoe, Fumimaro, 11-13
Konoe's 13
Korea 2, 4, 10, 22, 105
Korean 111
Kurita, Vice-Admiral Takao, 99
Kurita's 99
Kyushu 10, 22, 105

L
Lambulambu 71
Langstone, Frank, 12
Leander, HMNZS (ship), 38, 45, 56, 60, 62-64, 120, 130
Leese, Lieutenant-General Sir Oliver, 104, 125
Legasipi, 22
Leyte Gulf, 99, 100
Lockheed Hudson (medium bomber), 29, 43, 55, 110
Lockheed Ventura (medium bomber), 85, 96
London, 7, 12, 13, 35, 105, 113-118, 123-125, 131-134, 143
Lunga Point, 65
Luzon, 10, 22, 23, 99

M
MacArthur, General Douglas, 23, 36, 37, 41, 43, 61, 62, 66, 76, 82, 90, 105, 111
Mackay, Able-Seaman Malcolm, 26
Mackie, R. F., 97, 101, 102, 119, 124, 129, 130
Makambo, 61
Malaya, 1, 6, 10, 14, 15, 18, 19, 22, 24, 28, 115, 129, 133
Manchuria, 7, 38, 105
Maraquana Bay, 71
Marianas Islands, 2, 10, 22, 23, 62, 76, 98, 99
Marrakesh, 92
Mbennga Passage, 27
McCain, Admiral John R., 52
Melbourne, 2, 100, 113, 115, 116, 131-134
Mindanao, 10, 22, 23
Minhinnick, Gordon, 28

Mongolia, 10, 22
Monowai, HMNZS (ship), 26, 27, 38, 115, 130

N
Nagasaki, 107
Nagato, IJN (ship), 99
Nanking, 7, 10, 22
Nankivell, Colonel J. H., 47
New Caledonia, 2, 28, 30, 33, 34, 38, 44, 46, 49, 50, 52, 67, 69, 81, 93, 94, 127
New Hebrides, 2, 53
Nishimura, Vice-Admiral, 99
Nissan Island, 57, 68, 82-87, 89, 95, 96
North African theatre, 28, 67, 134
Noumea, 45, 47, 49, 51, 52, 65, 92, 118, 123
Nukumanu, 57, 68

O
Okinawa 10, 22, 99-101, 105
Olympic (Operation), 105, 125, 132
Ondonga, 60, 78, 81
Ozawa, Admiral Jisaburo, 98, 99

P
Palembang, 100, 109
Pallukula Airfield, 53
Papua New Guinea, 10, 22, 60, 95
Paraparaumu, 44
Paraso Bay, 71, 74
Patani, 18
Philippines 2, 4, 5, 10, 22, 23, 36, 37, 41, 62, 66, 82, 97, 99
Phillips, Rear-Admiral Sir Thomas, 15, 16
Plaine des Gaiacs, 49, 52
Pokonian Plantation, 84-89
Port Moresby, 2, 8, 10, 15, 22, 24, 33, 38, 39, 41
Potsdam, 107
Prince of Wales, HMS (ship), 13, 16, 17
Puriata River, 96

Puttick, Lieutenant-General Sir Edward, 27, 41, 43, 44, 46-48, 93-95, 104, 117-119, 122, 123

Q
Quadrant Conference, 66

R
Rabaul 22-24, 58, 60-62, 66, 75, 79, 81-83, 86, 87, 90, 95, 96
Rangoon, 10, 22, 23, 28
Rendova, 77
Repulse, HMS (ship), 13, 16, 17
Ribbentrop, Joachim von, 12
Roberts, Group Captain Geoffrey, 96
Roosevelt, President Franklin D., 9-14, 35, 36, 62, 92, 97, 117, 123, 131
Roskill, Commander S. W., 63, 114, 117, 118, 124
Ruahine Regiment, 48

S
Sabang, 98
Saigon, 10, 13, 16, 22
Sakishima Gunto, 100
Samoa, 24, 33, 38, 41, 61
San Bernadino Strait, 99
San Francisco, 5, 125
Saveke River, 79
Seeadler Harbour, 100
Seletar reservoirs, 21
Seoul, 10, 22
Shafroth, Rear-Admiral John, 92
Shanghai, 10, 22
Sidi Rezegh, 46
Sinclair-Burgess, Major-General W. L. H., 7
Singapore, 3, 6-10, 13-22, 24, 29, 32, 97, 104, 109, 110, 113, 115, 131, 133, 134
Singora, 10, 15, 18
Skinner, Ted, 50, 51, 66, 67, 69, 80, 81, 86, 89, 94, 119-123, 131
Soanotalu, 77-80
Solomon Islands, 1, 2, 24, 27, 33, 34, 37, 38, 41, 45, 52, 56-58, 60-62, 65,

66, 68-70, 76, 94, 96, 119, 130, 132.
Sourabaya, 98
Stronach, Captain J. F. B., 88
Suavanao, 57, 60, 68
Sumatra, 10, 20, 22, 97, 103
Suragao Strait, 99
Suva, 8, 26, 38

T
Talasea, 90
Tangalan Plantation, 84, 85, 87, 89
Tarawa, 82, 122, 129
Thailand, 10, 13, 14, 22, 23
Timbala Bay, 70, 71, 73, 74
Tingwon, 95
Tinian, 105, 107
Tobruk, 28, 35
Tonga, 2, 8, 46, 54, 55, 91, 119, 130
Tongatapu 8, 54
Torokina, 57, 60, 68, 81-83, 95
Torres Strait, 10, 22
Trobriand Islands, 61

U
Urago Straits, 108

V
Valentine (Mk III Infantry Tank), 87, 88, 128
Vandergrift, Major-General Alexander, 44, 45
Vella Lavella, 55, 57, 66-68, 70, 71, 75-77, 80-82, 84, 86, 87
Vichy France, 11, 13
Vladivostok 10, 22
Vonavona, 57, 60, 68
Vuranimala, 57, 60, 68

W
Waipukurau 97, 130
Wakefield, USS (ship), 44

Walinga, 95
Wallingford, Captain Sidney, 53
Warambari Bay, 70, 74, 75
Wavell, General Sir Archibald, 18-20, 23, 36, 114, 115
Wellington, 2, 8, 12, 27, 29, 31, 35, 37, 38, 44, 45, 47, 51, 54, 67, 95, 98, 103, 113-118, 121, 122, 125, 126, 131-134
West Virginia, USS (ship), 99
Wharton, USS (ship), 94
Whitehall 20
Wildish, Lieutenant D. B. H., 16
Wilkinson, Rear-Admiral T. S., 70, 83, 90

Y
Yamamoto, Admiral Isoruku, 14, 38, 39, 40, 45
Yamashita, General Tomoyuki, 15, 18-21
Yamato, IJN (ship), 99, 100
Yap, 10, 22
Yorktown, USS (ship), 39
Ysabel Channel, 95
Yugure, IJN (ship), 62
Yukikaze, IJN (ship), 62

Z
Zanzibar, 26
ZEAIRTAF (New Zealand Air Task Force), 96

About the author

Matthew Wright is a New Zealand writer with over thirty years professional experience as a published author and in publishing. He has qualifications in writing, music and anthropology among other fields, and holds multiple post-graduate degrees in history. He is a Fellow of the Royal Historical Society at University College, London.

Matthew Wright's New Zealand Military Series

Collect the set

www.ingramcontent.com/pod-product-compliance
Lightning Source LLC
Chambersburg PA
CBHW071412300426
44114CB00016B/2274